Trees

Frances Tenenbaum, Series Editor

 HOUGHTON MIFFLIN COMPANY

Boston • New York 1999

Trees

Easy Plants for More Beautiful Gardens

Produced by Storey Communications, Inc.
Pownal, Vermont

Taylor's Guide is a registered trademark of Houghton Mifflin
Company.

Library of Congress Cataloging-in-Publication Data is available.
ISBN 0-395-87332-0

Printed in the United States of America

WCT 10 9 8 7 6 5 4 3 2 1

CONTENTS

INTRODUCTION

Trees are the most dominant and permanent elements in the landscape. They determine the framework of the garden and dictate the amount of sun and shade that enter. A balance of evergreen and deciduous types alters the exposure from season to season as well as the color and texture of the whole. You can deepen the impact of trees by introducing bright spring or summer blossoms and rich autumn tints, exuberant and uplifting with their stunning displays. Yet it is summer foliage that makes the greatest impression on a garden scene. Leaf shape, size, and color work together for a variety of effects—green and comforting, colorful and lively, serene and cooling, dramatic or stately—vastly different among the scores of species and cultivars of ornamental trees.

The Landscape Role

In selecting a tree, pose a few questions to help define the role it will play in your landscape and to clarify your expectations. Will this tree be a companion to the architecture of your house, an aesthetic enhancement of your property? Are you looking for a natural element in an otherwise crowded urban area? Will it mark your property line or provide a barrier? Do you need this barrier for noise abatement, a privacy shield, or visual screening? Do you want a focal point, specimen, or accent plant?

Your purpose may be as simple and straightforward as breaking up the monotony of a barren new subdivision or introducing shade into a sunny front yard. Still, the questions continue. Are you looking for: a deciduous or an evergreen tree; heavy or light shade; shade for other plants, outdoor living, or indoor comfort? When your tree matures, it will cool the air around your house by several degrees in summer. A leafy canopy prevents heat from reflecting off pavement and keeps sunlight off walls and roofs, lowering the need for air-conditioning. Both evergreen and deciduous trees provide a cooling effect, but only deciduous trees let in winter sun for solar gain. When you are ready to get more specific, zero in on how you want your tree to look. Do you envision a particular leaf shape or type of bark? Both foliage and bark are important for the texture they contribute to an overall design. You will want to consider resident trees and nearby shrubs so the new tree is compatible. Do you have a particular shape in mind? Most trees are rounded, but there are spires, pyramids, umbrella shapes, and columnar types. Are you interested in a flowering canopy? In what season? What about scent and color? Is autumn leaf color a factor?

If you are beginning a search for a tree with a visual image in mind, try to expand your mental picture to include the appearance in all seasons, especially the pattern of bare branches if the tree is deciduous. If you are considering a flowering tree, you may or may not be satisfied with one that has a single outstanding season, then a ho-hum expression the rest of the year. Besides ornamental fall color and spring or summer blossoms, many trees offer rich tints on emerging spring foliage. Most of the trees included in this book are good looking year-round. Some have prominent bark and twig features or ornamental fruits that become winter focal points, especially when set against contrasting backgrounds.

The Planting Site

Before you decide on a specific tree, you must know exactly where you are going to plant it. Attempt to squarely face limitations that exist at your planting site. The site will determine the most critical elements about the tree—its size and shape, i.e., the height, spread, and habit. In the simplest terms, the site will determine whether you will plant a large or a small tree.

A small tree rarely grows out of control, combines well with shrubs, screens out unattractive views, makes an effective accent, and can be planted close to a structure and under other trees. A large tree dominates the landscape, provides shade, blocks vistas, and mitigates forceful winds. It may also demand a substantial seasonal cleanup, interfere with your neighbor's property, or overpower other plants.

For your tree to achieve its best form, it needs ample space. If it will face physical obstacles, consider substituting a narrower, lower cultivar or one with a less invasive root system. Evaluate the selected site for your tree with the following questions in mind:

- Is there ample head space for vertical and lateral growth? Determine the consequences if major limbs end up crossing property lines.

- Will there be enough soil in the root zone so that air and water can reach roots and so that shallow roots will not disturb other plants? When there is competition, the tree will dominate, even against a foundation.

- Are there any overhead or underground utility lines, septic tanks, leach fields, road signs, or other possible physical restraints?

- What type of root system does the tree have? Will it allow lawn or planting beds underneath?

A common myth about pruning perpetuates the notion that an ornamental tree can simply be hacked back whenever its branches begin to interfere with human activities. This practice is not good for either the health or the shape of most trees, since pruning cuts often invite destructive pathogens or insects and usually distort the natural beauty of a tree. Rather than choosing a tree that will grow too large for its site, opt for a named cultivar of the chosen species with a smaller growth habit, or dwarf or weeping characteristics. In some cases, you may simply have to choose a different type of tree, one shorter or narrower in habit. When you are evaluating your site, remember that it must be able to accommodate the mature canopy and root system. Planting too close to a structure or other trees inhibits sunlight and space necessary for a new tree to develop its natural shape.

The New Habitat

One key to success is to select a species from your local flora. A species native to your climate zone and naturally adapted to conditions of the planting site will grow easily. If you introduce a tree into an environment whose conditions are only marginally acceptable and very different from those in its native habitat, it will face intolerable stress. Your tree may struggle on for years, but inevitably it will be short lived.

Some species are less demanding than others, but all react to levels of annual rainfall and humidity, cold hardiness, and summer heat. A tree native to Zone 6, for example, may survive in warmer regions of Zone 5 until one or more severe winters cause fatal freeze damage, whereas trees native to Zone 5 are more likely to withstand abnormal cold. The same is true for other environmental factors. Plant only those species that are naturally adapted to the type of soil and pH in the new habitat. You may face a conundrum when a tree requires well-drained, nutrient-rich soil and you have clay. Though clay soils tend to be nutrient rich, most drain slowly and pose a risk to tree health unless the species is adapted to heavy soil. Note whether your selection is vigorous enough to withstand other difficult environmental factors, such as polluted air or salt spray. Some trees can survive many conditions but will appear dwarfed and unhealthy, offering little in the way of aesthetic enhancement.

Don't forget to evaluate exposure when planting your new tree. A shade-loving and ascending Japanese maple, for instance, may do quite well under the protection of existing low shade until its branches rise above surrounding shrubs and its tender foliage burns. Does that mean you will not be able to plant a Japanese maple in a chosen spot? Not at all, only that you need to select a sun-tolerant variety if the eventual height will exceed that of other shrubs or small trees in its vicinity.

The Larger Picture

It is always a good idea to check your neighborhood to see which trees thrive there. By choosing a variety of trees, you add diversity to the area around you. Diversity strengthens the ecology of the region, fostering more wildlife while promoting healthy plants that are more disease, pest, and drought tolerant. Lack of diversity fosters insect and disease problems.

Creating diversity can also be a method of blending your new landscape into the surrounding natural scene. Look past your immediate site to what lies beyond. The visual boundaries may be merely on adjacent properties, or they may extend to hills in the distance. To create enduring beauty, set your part of the picture in harmony and scale within the whole and bequeath a celebration of trees to future generations.

WHITE FIR

Abies concolor

Zones: 4–7

Type: Evergreen

Light: Full sun to part shade

Size: 30–80 ft. tall, 15–40 ft. wide

Form: Conical

Growth Rate: Slow to moderate

Interest: Flat, blue-green needles; purplish cones

Slow growing and compact when young, white fir matures into a majestic, conical tree. Pale, blue-green, 2-inch needles and strongly horizontal branches give it a silvery appearance and elegant symmetry, the shape of a perfect Christmas tree. The bark on young trees is smooth and gray while on older trees, it is paler and becomes thick and furrowed. Tall, mature white firs produce purplish or olive-colored cones that sit like candles on upper branches, then shatter as they ripen.

HOW TO GROW

White fir withstands cold, rugged conditions and it ranks among the best conifers for the East and Midwest. It tolerates limited drought and does best in slightly acidic, well-drained soil in climates with some humidity. Avoid heavy clay soil or windy sites. Where rain is scarce or undependable, water moderately. Give white fir some shade where summers are hot. Select a planting site carefully to allow for white fir's eventual height. Keep a circle around the base free of vegetation and covered with mulch. Each year, enlarge the circle so it is at least 1 foot beyond the ends of the branches and replenish the mulch. In warm regions, spider mites can be a problem. Control with applications of insecticidal soap once a month from late spring to late summer.

LANDSCAPE USE

This stately tree makes an excellent specimen in a large lawn where it can stand alone to be admired from all sides. It does not respond well to pruning or shearing, so give it plenty of room where it will not interfere with views or other landscaping. Contrast its formal, blue-green foliage with nearby stands of darker evergreens such as the black-green Nordman fir or a group of graceful, giant arborvitaes. Keep it out of heavy shade, however, where it grows extremely slowly and loses its compact form.

Top Choices

- *A.* 'Candicans' is strikingly silver-white, one of the palest-colored conifers.

- *A. koreana,* Korean fir, is a good choice for difficult urban sites because it tolerates pollution and compacted soil better than most firs. Its growth and smaller size (to 30 feet) make it suitable for smaller gardens.

PLANT AND WATER WELL

1 In spring or fall, dig a hole as deep as the rootball and twice as wide. Lift the rootball—do not lift the tree by its trunk—and set it on the bottom of the hole.

2 Untie the burlap, but if it is made of natural jute you can leave it to hold the soil around the roots. Remove any plastic and wire cord or wrapping.

3 Make several cuts through the burlap, from bottom to top, thus allowing the roots to expand more quickly.

4 Fill the hole with the soil you dug out. Thinly cover feeder roots on the top of the rootball, but avoid the bottom of the trunk where it begins to flare out.

5 Water well; cover the soil with a 2- to 4-inch-thick layer of compost or finely chipped bark in a 3- to 5-foot-wide circle.

SMALL MAPLES

Acer

Zones: 5–9

Type: Deciduous

Light: Full sun to part shade

Size: 8–30 ft. tall, 8–30 ft. wide

Form: Varies by species

Growth Rate: Slow to moderate

Interest: Lobed leaves that vary in size, shape, and color; decorative fruits, bark, and fall foliage

Small maples are treasures in the landscape, indispensable where garden space is limited. Their attractive foliage and fall fruits (wing-shaped samaras) bring several seasons of beauty. Many small maples combine exquisite leaf shape, color, and texture with beautiful bark and graceful form, adding beauty to any place they're planted. Small maples stand out everywhere, especially near water, where reflections double their effect.

HOW TO GROW

Small maples favor moist, well-drained soil, rich in organic matter, though some such as trident maple require acidic soil. Light afternoon shade is recommended in areas with hot summers to reduce leaf damage from sunlight. Plant in slightly acidic soil, away from windy sites or places. Seasonal chores include pruning to shape in winter while the tree is dormant and fertilizing lightly in spring.

LANDSCAPE USE

Small maples make popular additions to Japanese and rock gardens. Their size makes them a perfect fit for pocket-sized gardens, containers, courtyards, and patios. Most also make ideal specimen trees to accent lawns or buildings. Try combining them with dwarf and columnar conifers for a striking contrast.

Top Choices

- *A. palmatum,* Japanese maple, is a nicely shaped tree with deeply lobed, attractively colored foliage. Cultivars vary enormously in habit, from broad-spreading domes to dwarf hummocks. 'Bloodgood', 'Butterfly', and 'Deshojo' are three outstanding cultivars. Zones 5 to 9.

- *A. japonicum,* full-moon maple, is similar to Japanese maple but slightly hardier with broad, many-lobed soft green leaves that turn bright scarlet and yellow in fall. 'Aconitifolium' (fernleaf maple) has magnificent fall color. Zones 5 to 7.

- *A. palmatum* 'Dissectum', laceleaf Japanese maple, has delicate, deeply cut leaves in green, red, or purple. 'Green Lace', 'Crimson Queen', and 'Garnet' have green, red, and reddish purple foliage, respectively.

OTHER SMALL MAPLES

A. buergeranum, trident maple, bears shiny, three-lobed green leaves, spectacular yellowish orange to rosy maroon in fall. It is a slow-growing, highly prized small shade tree that withstands some drought. An excellent street or lawn tree, it is attractive even in winter, when the peeling orange-brown bark is most visible. Zones 5 to 9.

A. griseum, paperbark maple, is a favorite among fanciers of specialty plants and looks very unlike a maple. Its outstanding feature is thin, cinnamon-colored, curling and peeling bark. Three-part green leaves, which need protection from intense summer sun, have a silvery underside in spring and summer; in fall they turn orange and scarlet. Few trees create such a sensation. Zones 4 to 8.

A. tataricum subsp. *ginnala,* amur maple, is good for a screening hedge, patio tree, or container plant. It is one of the hardiest and most durable of the genus, tolerating wind and drought and heavy and alkaline soil. It performs best in ordinary, moist garden conditions. Its fragrant spring flowers are upstaged by the rosy red summer fruits and richly colored, three-lobed leaves in autumn. It grows best in full sun. Zones 3 to 9.

LARGE MAPLES
Acer

Zones: 3–9

Type: Deciduous

Light: Full sun to part shade

Size: 50–100 ft. tall, 30–60 ft. wide

Form: Rounded and spreading

Growth Rate: Moderate

Interest: Lobed leaves vary in size, shape, and color; decorative fruits and bark

Large maples long ago won their place in the landscape for their sheer beauty and practical shade. These trees perform best and are longest lived when you choose a species well suited to your climate, soil, and site. Some of the best are not only easy-care but gloriously painted each autumn in orange, red, and gold foliage. There is a large maple perfect for every region and growing condition.

HOW TO GROW

Plant large maples in moist, fertile, well-drained soil with ample organic matter in a site with plenty of room. Water regularly for the first two years and during dry periods thereafter to avoid leaf scorch. Avoid planting maples near paved areas where their shallow roots can heave pavement. Many large maples are damaged by road salt and pollution and should not be used as street trees.

LANDSCAPE USE

Large maples make some of the best shade trees for large yards. Many species, such as red and sugar maples, offer stunning fall colors and become more ruggedly beautiful with age. Memories of swinging from their branches will stay with children long after they have grown.

Top Choices

- *A. rubrum,* red maple, grows quickly to 40 to 80 feet and spreads half as wide. 'Red Sunset' explodes in orange and red color in fall; 'October Glory' colors late and is preferred in the South, while 'Autumn Flame' bears a heavy canopy of smallish leaves that are among the earliest to color. Zones 3 to 9.

- *A. saccharum,* sugar maple, is the flagship of landscape trees in the East and Midwest with its boldly colored fall foliage. 'Bonfire' is fast growing with orange-red fall color. It tolerates urban conditions better than other sugar maples. The leaves of 'Legacy' resist tearing in the wind, making it a favorite for breezy places like the Midwest. 'Caddo' is superior on the Great Plains for its hardiness, heat tolerance, and drought resistance. Deep maroon fall color develops late in the season. Zones 4 to 8.

MAPLES TO AVOID

Not all maples can be recommended as the best trees for the landscape. Some are weedy or invasive trees, while others have weak wood and are prone to storm damage.

- Silver maple, *A. saccharinum,* is a widely planted shade tree with attractive leaves. It has weak wood and a branching pattern that makes it easily damaged in storms.

- Norway maple, *A. platanoides,* is an aggressive species that has become a weed tree in parts of the South and East, where it is threatening stands of sugar maple and beech. In yards, it casts shade too dense for lawns or planting beds to grow underneath.

- Box elder, *A. negundo,* is a common, rapid-growing, native tree. Its brittle wood makes it prone to storm damage while its weedy nature makes it a nuisance.

RED HORSE CHESTNUT

Aesculus x *carnea*

Zones: 5–7

Type: Deciduous

Light: Full sun

Size: 35 ft. tall, 20 ft. wide

Form: Round headed

Growth Rate: Moderate

Interest: Large, palmate leaves; scarlet spring flowers; buckeye seeds

Red horse chestnut is a medium-sized tree, stunning in full bloom, with scarlet flowers. Its showy red panicles stand up like candelabras at the branch tips in late spring. Each dark green leaf has five to seven leaflets joined palmately, each up to 10 inches long. Pear-shaped fruits hang from trees in fall, then split open to reveal knobby brown seeds. These shiny "buckeyes," somewhat toxic if ingested, are attractive in fall flower arrangements.

HOW TO GROW

Grow red horse chestnut in full sun. It is more drought tolerant than horse chestnut (one of its parents) and is less susceptible to leaf scorch. If summer rain is scarce, give it supplemental watering to speed growth and keep the large canopy richly green. This tree needs well-drained soil with a pH below 6.5. (See page 107, "Testing Your Soil."). It is best to plant only young trees, and these in late fall or early spring during dormancy. Choose container-grown or balled-and-burlapped plants.

LANDSCAPE USE

Spectacular in the landscape, red horse chestnut can be planted singly or in groups. Three or more make an impressive stand along a fence or property line, spaced 25 feet apart. In a lawn, cover the root zone with a circle of mulch to minimize the competition between turf and the naturally shallow feeder roots. Avoid planting this tree near a patio or street, since faded flowers, seeds, and seedpods are a litter problem. This is a useful shade tree wherever space is limited. Shade-loving foliage plants make suitable companions, but keep flowering plants beyond the heavy shade of red horse chestnut's canopy.

Top Choices

- A. 'Briotii' is a popular variety with rose-red flowers 8 to 10 inches above branch tips.

- A. 'Ft. McNair' develops a dense canopy with 6- to 8-inch, dark pink blossoms.

- A. 'O'Neill' is similar to 'Briotii' with deep green leaves and flowers an even darker red.

WATERING TECHNIQUES

To keep water from damaging the crown of red horse chestnut, construct a shallow watering basin that will distribute water to both the rootball and the surrounding soil.

1 Make a circular mound of soil a few inches high about a foot from the trunk, and another just beyond the branch tips.

2 Keep the area between the mounds under the tree well mulched with organic matter.

3 As the tree grows, move the watering basin outward. Most of the feeder roots will be at or near the drip line and in the top 2 feet of soil. Check soil moisture content every few weeks. Let the top few inches dry out but keep the deeper soil moist. Water slowly, applying only as much as the soil can absorb.

SERVICEBERRY
Amelanchier

Zones: 4–9

Type: Deciduous

Light: Full sun to part shade

Size: 15–25 ft. tall, 10–15 ft. wide

Form: Rounded; single or multistemmed

Growth Rate: Moderate

Interest: Dark green leaves with rich fall color; white spring flowers; edible berries

Serviceberry can be described as a small tree or large shrub—a single- or multistemmed plant that most often grows 15 to 25 feet tall and half as wide. Also called juneberry and shadblow, it stays good looking throughout all four seasons. Abundant early-spring flowers, tasty summer berries, brilliant fall color, and delicate winter tracery make it an outstanding addition to the garden. Young leaves are either fuzzy and grayish green or smooth and bronze, depending on the species and variety. In autumn, serviceberry revels in glorious shades of red, yellow, and orange. Deep green summer color is highlighted with clusters of reddish purple edible fruits—until the birds discover them.

HOW TO GROW

Serviceberry is a versatile and long-lived tree. It prefers moist, well-drained, acidic soil but will grow in almost any type of soil and withstand severe heat, intense cold, and some drought. Its branches are somewhat brittle and may break in high winds. Prune out damaged limbs and unwanted suckers that rise from the base. Thin to the strongest four to eight stems for the most vigorous upright growth. This tree can take a year to adjust to a new situation. Try to plant small, young trees, because it takes older plants much longer to recover from transplanting.

LANDSCAPE USE

Nearly all serviceberry species blend in easily among shrubs to add a layer under taller deciduous trees. In a narrow space or along a street, train it as a single-trunked tree or choose an upright cultivar such as 'Cumulus'. For wider branching and more bulk, allow several stems to develop or plant a broader-spreading variety such as 'Strata'. Its horizontal branches and open canopy let light filter through to perennials below.

Top Choices

- *A.* x *grandiflora* is taller and has long, pendant clusters of large flowers and fruits and exceptional fall color. 'Autumn Brilliance' is one of the best for a colorful autumn show.

- *A.* 'Cumulus' has a vigorous, upright habit.

- *A.* 'Strata' has blush-white flowers on spreading branches.

Taylor's Tips

TRANSITION TO A WOODLAND

As a native of woodland edges across North America, serviceberry is one of the best transition plants between formal or open areas around the house and a natural woodland beyond. Since it lacks a formal shape, it is especially useful for difficult outlying areas.

In full flower in spring, the white blossoms glimmer against a shadowy, forested backdrop or beside the dark water of a pond or lake. If your soil is wet or swampy, choose the shrubbier *A. canadensis* (often called shadblow); if it is dry or rocky, plant *A. laevis* or *A. arborea* (called juneberry).

EASY CARE

Though insects and diseases often visit serviceberry, they rarely are serious enough to warrant treatment. Fertilize only if the soil is poor, and then only minimally to avoid excessive tender growth susceptible to fire blight disease. Named cultivars, such as warmly colored 'Autumn Sunset', heavy-flowering 'Ballerina', and brightly hued 'Princess Diana', generally have the fewest problems. They are available from local and mail-order nurseries.

STRAWBERRY TREE
Arbutus unedo

Zones: 8–9

Type: Evergreen

Light: Full sun

Size: 5–20 ft. tall, 20 ft. wide

Form: Multistemmed with wide-spreading crown

Growth Rate: Slow

Interest: Glossy green leaves; pale flowers in fall; soft red fruits; attractive bark

Strawberry tree becomes increasingly attractive with age as it twists and spirals and the reddish brown bark furrows and shreds. The glossy, dark green foliage forms a thick, mounding canopy that withstands wind and drought. Throughout fall and early winter, urn-shaped white to pale pink flowers dangle in small clusters from reddish twigs while fruits from last year's blossoms mature. The yellow and red strawberry-like drupes (edible, though bland and mushy) persist for many weeks.

HOW TO GROW
Virtually pest- and disease-free, strawberry tree thrives in acidic or alkaline soil, from coastal sand to heavy clay, in lawns or raised beds. Its toughness and drought tolerance make it one of the most valuable small trees

on the West Coast. A good choice for urban sites, it is not bothered by high heat, smog, or compacted soil. Prune off suckers that sprout from the base as soon as they appear. If its shade is too dense, selectively thin out a few branches to open up the canopy and allow sun to filter through to plants below. Unless trained to grow on a single stem, it usually develops several trunks.

LANDSCAPE USE

Strawberry tree is one of the best small trees for a hot, dry site in mild climates, and one of the most sculptural when it is trained to develop multiple trunks. Choose a site near a patio or walkway— where the rough, gnarled trunks deserve to be viewed close up—and spacious enough to accommodate the low, wide-spreading canopy. In dry climates, plant strawberry tree with other tender evergreens such as ceanothus and rock roses (*Cistus*). Where rain is abundant, add contrasting forms and autumn color with small maples such as Japanese, amur, and full-moon maples.

Top Choices

- *A.* 'Compacta' grows 5 feet tall with deep green leaves and flowers and fruits nearly continuously.

- *A.* 'Elfin King' grows to 10 feet tall and bears plentiful flowers and fruits.

INCOMPARABLE PACIFIC MADRONE

A larger tree than the strawberry tree, the madrone (*A. menziesii*) stands alone among Pacific Coast natives in incomparable beauty. The mahogany-red outer bark peels away in sheets or flakes to reveal a smooth, cinnamon-hued underlayer. The madrone commonly develops one or more stems, bright leathery leaves, and drooping of bell-shaped blossoms, then orange-red fruits relished by birds.

Plant madrone in full or part sun in a site that has good drainage and is protected from cold, drying winds. Transplant it from a small container or tube, keep moist until established, then water infrequently or not at all.

If low temperatures kill the top growth, it may come back from the roots, but it rarely survives extended cold below 5° F.

Bright berry clusters complement the glossy foliage of the strawberry tree.

RIVER BIRCH
Betula nigra

Zones: 4–9

Type: Deciduous

Light: Full or part sun

Size: 40–70 ft. tall, 40–60 ft. wide

Form: Pyramidal to oval or rounded

Growth Rate: Moderate to fast

Interest: Dark green leaves that yellow in fall; brown, dangling spring catkins; peeling bark

Unlike other birches, which often succumb to heat and dry conditions, river birch tolerates considerable stress. In youth, its pale, ragged bark peels in curling flakes. On older trees, the bark turns darker gray or black and ridged.

HOW TO GROW

Rich, fertile loam is the ideal soil for birches. It readily holds moisture, yet is well drained. Ideally, the soil at ground level should be shaded to keep it cool and moist. Adaptable river birch, however, will tolerate clay and some standing water as well as heat and short periods of drought. Though it will not thrive in arid conditions, it tolerates dry soil better than other birches. It must have acidic conditions with a pH below 6.5, or leaves will turn yellow from chlorosis. Plant all birches where you don't need to prune to control normal growth. Pruning cuts and other bark wounds cause serious problems from fungal infections and insect invasions. River birch is the most disease-free birch and is resistant to the bronze birch borer. This insect is attracted to stressed plants, usually those growing in hostile conditions and often suffering from drought. Commonly planted *B. pendula*, European white birch, suffers serious borer damage and consequently is often short lived.

LANDSCAPE USE

Always good looking, river birch is easy to use in the landscape. It makes an excellent lawn tree spaced at least 20 to 30 feet from a house or structure to allow for its mature trunk girth and wide-spreading crown. As with other birch species, it is most attractive planted in groups. Though it becomes a large tree, river birch is a good choice for planting on banks, especially near streams, to control erosion. It is one of the best trees to use in low-lying areas that are swampy during winter thaw and spring rains. If pruning is necessary, do it in summer, because river birch "bleeds" heavily.

Top Choice

- *B.* 'Heritage', a new cultivar, is larger and more vigorous than the species and is valued for its apricot-cream bark that remains pale as the tree ages. Leaf surfaces are glossy green above and shimmering silver below. In fall, color fades to a dull yellow.

TROUBLE-FREE WHITESPIRE BIRCH

Graceful and airy, white birches are popular choices for lawn and landscape trees. Of all the white birches, Whitespire birch (*B. platyphylla* var. *japonica* 'Whitespire') is the most heat tolerant and trouble-free. It is also one of the few resistant to the fatal attraction of the bronze birch borer.

This lissome, chalky white tree grows quickly to a 20-foot spire, then at a moderate pace to 40 feet, a suitable size for most gardens. If you have ample room, plant a grove of five or more with 10 to 15 feet between trees. Otherwise, group two or three together in the same planting hole.

Whitespire birch is best in Zones 4 to 7 in rich, well-drained loam or sandy soil with protection from strong winds. During dry spells, water to keep at least the top 2 feet of soil evenly moist.

EUROPEAN HORNBEAM
Carpinus betulus

Zones: 5–8

Type: Deciduous

Light: Full sun to part shade

Size: 50 ft. tall, 40 ft. wide

Form: Oval to rounded

Growth Rate: Slow to moderate

Interest: Dark green leaves, yellow to red in fall; dangling catkins in spring

European hornbeam develops an outline that never fails to attract attention. In youth, it maintains an oval shape; with age, the upper canopy becomes more rounded with pendulous outer branches. Several varieties grow in shrubby forms, maturing into either egg or pyramidal shapes with dense, vertical branches. In spring, lime green catkins dangle below the leaves. In autumn, yellow leaves slowly fade to brown and often remain on the tree for months.

HOW TO GROW

Hornbeam is an undemanding tree. It does best in cold climates but thrives in a wide range of ordinary soil and conditions. It has few pest and disease problems and is not troubled by urban pollution. For the best possible site, choose a location protected from strong winds. Trim hornbeam hedges in late summer or early autumn to prevent sap from bleeding. On tree forms, prune out crossing and errant branches at their base. These will otherwise detract from the well-balanced winter silhouette.

LANDSCAPE USE

European hornbeam fills many roles in the landscape. Selected varieties, such as 'Columnaris', are small enough to plant in groups for interest in a large lawn or alone close to buildings. It is effective as a screen, even in winter with its branching dense and close to the ground. Hornbeam is widely used as a tall hedge plant since it responds well to shearing. It can also be used for pleaching (intertwining branches) to establish a dense arbor or create an intimate, tree-lined pathway. Though not highly colorful in autumn, European hornbeam remains handsome in winter. When mature, its smooth gray bark has a rugged heftiness that is attractive bare or rimed with frost.

Top Choices

- C. 'Columnaris', a slow-growing variety with a narrow, spirelike shape, is suitable for windbreaks, hedges, and screens.

- C. 'Fastigiata' has a more broad shape than 'Columnaris' but is still more narrow and upright than the species. It is pest- and disease-free as well as drought tolerant.

AN AMERICAN RELATIVE

Known by several names (blue beech, water beech, ironwood, and musclewood), the American hornbeam (*C. caroliniana*) is slower growing and much smaller in habit than its taller European relative. The common names arise from its bright green, beechlike leaves, the great strength of its wood, and the slate gray bark that undulates in smooth ridges, giving trunk and branches the appearance of sinewy muscles.

American hornbeam is also more rounded and domelike than European hornbeam, and makes a good choice for backyard play and climbing. Since growth is slow, however, you will need to plan ahead. For a good start, plant it balled-and- burlapped (see page 11) in fertile soil with some shade from taller trees. When young, it can be trained to develop low, horizontal branching for strong support and easy climbing. After ten years, it should be large enough for small children. Zones 3 to 9.

SHAGBARK HICKORY
Carya ovata

Zones: 4–8

Type: Deciduous

Light: Full to part sun

Size: 100 ft. tall, 40 ft. wide

Form: Tall, narrow, with vertical crown and open branching

Growth Rate: Slow to moderate

Interest: Large pinnate leaves; edible nuts; rough, shaggy bark

When you plant a shagbark hickory, you are planting a tree for future generations. It lives for more than a hundred years as a stalwart element in a landscape, providing high, filtered shade so important in hot summer climates, both humid and dry. Hickory leaves grow 12 to 14 inches long with five glossy green leaflets and turn rich golden brown in autumn. The rough, shaggy outline is beautifully picturesque in winter.

HOW TO GROW

Hickory requires no special care. It grows best in deep loam soil, but will tolerate clay. Trees tend to remain trouble-free, but insect and disease problems may turn up if trees become stressed from drought. As a group, trees in the *Carya* genus dislike having their roots disturbed, so plant hickory either balled-and-burlapped or from a small container while it is very young and has a small root system. No pruning is required. If you do need to remove any crossing or damaged small branches, set a few aside. In small quantities the wood makes a nice addition to fires for flavoring outdoor cooking.

LANDSCAPE USE

Plant shagbark hickory where you can appreciate its distinctive surface and contrast it with smoother trees such as yellowwood, flowering crab apple, or deciduous magnolia. Rough hickory bark flakes off in thick, often long, vertical plates that loosen and curl first at the top and bottom. Allow loose bark to peel and drop, then clean it up if your tree is planted in a lawn. Though usually grown on large properties and in spacious lawns, don't overlook hickory if you have a small garden. It can prosper in narrow sites as long as there is enough vertical space.

Best from Seeds

In natural forests, nut trees grow from seeds. Growth is most vigorous when trees are not transplanted. All species in the *Carya* genus develop a taproot that often grows faster below ground than the stem does above ground. These trees become slightly stunted when grown for long periods in nursery cans; they lose much of their root systems when they are dug up from fields. Hickory and pecan grow best when planted from seeds.

A STATELY ALTERNATIVE

Related to shagbark hickory, the pecan (*C. illinoinensis*) is a broad-canopied tree native to the Midwest and South. In long, hot summers, it bears heavy nut crops. Where summers are shorter, it produces no nuts but still serves as an important, stately shade tree. Too large for typical suburban lots, it needs plenty of room to spread and deep, loose soil for its large taproot. Trees grow slowly, reaching 60 to 80 feet. Trees of great age can reach 150 feet.

Pecans generally tolerate heavy, poor soil, but they are more robust and long lived in well-drained loam. If you expect nuts, fertilize lightly each spring with nitrogen spread over a wide area reaching just beyond the drip line. For healthier, more productive trees, leave lower branches in place. As with other nut trees, plant pecans where falling nuts won't cause problems. Your Cooperative Extension Service agent can advise you on the best nut-producing varieties for your climate. Zones 5 to 9.

ATLAS CEDAR
Cedrus atlantica

Zones: 6–9

Type: Evergreen

Light: Full sun

Size: 60 ft. tall, 30–40 ft. wide

Form: Stiff and angular in youth; flat topped and spreading in maturity

Growth Rate: Fast when young, then slow

Interest: Bluish to light green needles; 2- to 3-in. round cones

The shape of young atlas cedars varies considerably from one tree to another, but the striking beauty remains constant. This is a regal tree with stiff, irregularly spaced branches that tend to culminate in a spiky crown in youth. Older trees, which become quite picturesque, are broader and denser, the long limbs more horizontal than vertical. Short, sharp needles are carried in whorled clusters on tiny spurs varying in color from olive green to an almost iridescent, pale blue.

HOW TO GROW

Plant atlas cedar in a sunny site in deep, well-drained soil. Loam is best, but it will tolerate clay with good drainage or sand with frequent moisture. Established trees can tolerate drought and pollution, making them good choices for urban areas. Trees should be no taller than 2 feet at planting time; larger ones may not transplant well. Give atlas cedar at least 20 feet to spread on all sides, and protect it from winter wind, which will turn needles brown and may break limbs. If breaking occurs, prune carefully to avoid unnatural branching patterns. Allow only one central leader to develop; when heading back the side branches take care not to ruin the tree's natural shape.

LANDSCAPE USE

Despite its awkward, angular early growth, mature atlas cedar is one of the grandest of all conifers. It is more of a specimen than a shade tree, so take time to evaluate your planting site when selecting this tree. Check needle color at purchase time and choose the shade that will blend best into your landscape. Select a site in an open, prominent location unobstructed by other trees. For many years, the lowest branches remain attached, then drop as trees age. The atlas cedar looks best if these low limbs are left in place as long as possible.

About the Cones

The barrel-shaped cones that grow on the upper branches of atlas cedar become quite resinous and shatter in the second or third year after they form. They are quite pretty on the tree—bluish when young, then pale green and brown as they ripen. Don't plan on collecting any of these cones, though. They are never intact by the time they hit the ground.

COLOR AND ARTISTIC FORM

From a distance, the shimmering sheen of silver atlas cedar (C. 'Argentea') looks like a dusting of snow sitting lightly on the ascending branches. Foliage of blue atlas cedar (C. 'Glauca') is similar but more bluish gray. These two varieties are often confused and may not be labeled correctly at a nursery. Make your selection based on the needle color. Individual blue atlas cedars range from pale blue to greenish blue.

The most unusual form of this species is the most impressive. Weeping blue atlas cedar (C. 'Glauca Pendula') is a specialized grafted form that must be staked or supported on a trellis to develop any height. The central, thin trunk and all branches "weep" as they hang from their supports in cascades of thin, delicate tresses, creating a spectacular living sculpture. The form each tree takes depends on the staking method and the training you give it.

HACKBERRY
Celtis occidentalis

Zones: 3–9

Type: Deciduous

Light: Full sun

Size: 40–60 ft. tall, 30–40 ft. wide

Form: Pyramidal to spreading

Growth Rate: Moderate to fast

Interest: Medium green, oval leaves; reddish purple berries in fall

Similar to elm, but smaller and resistant to Dutch elm disease, hackberry is a good, shade-producing substitute. Hackberry roots grow deeper than elm's, so you can easily plant a lawn or ornamental garden underneath without the problem of protruding surface roots. The fruits of hackberry are reddish to purple and very sweet but have a single, tooth-shattering seed. They are attractive mainly to birds, so planting a hackberry is a good way to attract them to your yard in fall.

HOW TO GROW

A hackberry tree will grow nearly anywhere—in soil that is acidic or alkaline, wet or dry, compacted or well drained. It tolerates urban pollution, desert heat, and wind. Easy-care and long lived (over one hundred years), this is a tree that you can plant and forget as soon as it is established. It is best to plant a hackberry either from a container or balled-and-burlapped; it may be unsuccessful planted bareroot. When planting, stake your tree if it will be subjected to gusty winds. (See "Staking a Tree" at right.) After planting, keep the rootball and the surrounding area moist.

LANDSCAPE USE

Hackberry's deep roots make it safe for planting near buildings and sidewalks as well as in lawns. The presence of corky ridges along the trunk of a mature tree is a peculiarity that makes interesting close-up viewing. However, you will want to keep the tree far enough away from a patio or deck to prevent fruit litter from becoming a nuisance. Thriving in its large native region east of the Rocky Mountains, common hackberry also grows easily in all climate zones of the West.

Top Choices

- C. 'Magnifica' is a hybrid with all the good traits of the species and more. The plants are extremely drought tolerant and thrive near the shore or in the city. Zones 5 to 9.

- C. 'Prairie Pride' bears fewer fruits than the species, a plus for those who don't like to clean up after their landscape.

STAKING A TREE

Most trees grow better without staking. Only stake if your young tree is particularly floppy or in a very windy location. Before staking, remove the nursery stake. Then:

❶ Drive two sturdy 2 x 2 inch stakes into undisturbed soil, beyond the rootball, and deep enough so they will not move. Place them about 12 inches from the trunk, positioning so they are in line with prevailing winds. Use stakes just tall enough to anchor just below the lowest branches.

❷ Loop a broad, flexible material around the tree and tie it loosely enough to allow the tree to sway 4 to 6 inches in the wind.

❸ In six months, remove the ties. If the tree needs further support, replace the ties, lowering their position on the trunk and trimming stakes as needed. Remove them after one year.

KATSURA TREE
Cercidiphyllum japonicum

Zones: 4–8

Type: Deciduous

Light: Full sun

Size: 40–80 ft. tall, 25–40 ft. wide

Form: Pyramidal to spreading

Growth Rate: Fast

Interest: Round, bluish green leaves, yellow-orange in fall

In autumn, as its leaves blend soft oranges and buttery yellows with splashes of red, the katsura emits an elusive fragrance. One day the scent may be unmistakably like ripe apples, but the next it becomes more tantalizing and reminiscent of strawberries or caramelized sugar. On some trees, multiple trunks rise with horizontal or ascending branches like a colossal shrub, graceful and pleasing to the eye. Katsura is one of the fastest-growing trees under cultivation, but it rarely exceeds 70 to 80 feet tall.

HOW TO GROW
Hardy and pest-free, katsura tree grows quickly and easily from seeds. Young trees are easy to transplant, but those only a few years old are often slow to recover from having their roots disturbed. Keep transplants well

watered and mulched for two to three years until well established. Rich, slightly acidic loam that is well drained and supplied with regular water in full sun suits it best. Autumn color is less pronounced in alkaline soils. For consistently fast growth, keep the soil moist, especially when the tree is young, and protect it from constant winds. Sustain its normal fast growth with a light, annual application of a slow-release balanced fertilizer in spring.

LANDSCAPE USE

Always good looking, katsura tree is a natural choice for a landscape focal point. It creates a majestic alley when planted in double rows 30 feet apart or a stately grove in groups of three or more. In a smaller garden, keep other plants at least 10 feet away from the base so as not to detract from the beautiful shape.

Top Choice

- C. *j.* 'Pendula', weeping katsura, is a specialized form that must be grafted onto a rootstock. This fast-growing, small tree reaches only 15 to 25 feet. The vertical stem and pendulous branches never attain much girth, endowing the tree with a delicacy that is truly fountainlike. The slender branches and blue-green foliage on this weeping tree must also have a position in full sun with protection from strong winds for best performance.

SCREENING FOR PRIVACY

To provide privacy for outdoor living areas or upper-story rooms, a fast-growing tree makes a desirable screen. Despite its deciduous character, katsura tree is an excellent choice for a privacy screen. Its outstanding foliage and handsome winter silhouette supply it with a year-round appeal, and its dense branching provides a thicket that blocks out views. The effect is most distinctive and the screening most complete when the branches are left growing on the trunk at ground level.

Although it may seem like a contradiction, seed-grown plants will actually provide a screen faster than transplants. Since katsura tree grows as easily from seeds as do most garden vegetables, it is possible to have a 20-foot-tall screen only five years after seeding.

Planted in spring, a seed-grown tree can reach 5 feet in one growing season. Sow seeds where the tree is to grow, or transplant within a few weeks of sprouting.

EASTERN REDBUD
Cercis canadensis

Zones: 5–9

Type: Deciduous

Light: Full sun to part shade

Size: 20–35 ft. tall, 25–35 ft. wide

Form: Spreading to rounded

Growth Rate: Moderate

Interest: Heart-shaped, glossy green leaves; mauve-pink spring flowers; flat, pealike pods

Redbud stands out as one of the most delightful early-blooming trees. Purplish red buds strung like bright jewels along black, furrowed branches open to reveal small, pink to lilac blossoms that look like small sweet peas. Throughout spring and summer, glossy leaves flutter on long petioles, casting light and filtered shade. In fall, the leaves turn golden yellow. Flattened seedpods hang from the branches throughout winter. This is a short-lived tree, declining after twenty to thirty years.

HOW TO GROW

In a shrub border or woodland, train redbud to be multistemmed by cutting back the central leader of a young plant. Stems will spread broadly, with numerous branches increasing the potential for heavy blossoming. In a patio or small yard, opt for a single trunk with upward-angling branches for space to garden underneath. For a sculptured focal point, prune the lower branches of two or three well-spaced trunks. Redbud adapts to nearly every situation except heavy clay, constantly wet soil, or severe drought. Sandy, well-drained loam is ideal for its deep rooting habit. Vigorous growth sometimes shades interior branches, causing them to die back. Thin the canopy to allow for additional filtered sunlight.

LANDSCAPE USE

One of the most dazzling spring sights is a row of redbuds in full bloom. Though each blossom is small, their numbers are virtually countless, giving the effect of a veil-like mist. Redbud is a popular understory tree near the edge of a woodland garden, but it is also a choice plant for a prominent spot outside a living room window, where you can view its showy display on crisp spring days. Redbud lends itself to an anchor position in a small garden or large bed of bulbs.

Top Choices

- C. 'Silver Cloud' grows just 12 feet tall and has fewer flowers than the species. Its foliage is spectacular in colors of green, white, and pink. Grow it in light shade to protect the delicate leaves from sunscald.

- C. 'Forest Pansy' is a striking tree in blossom (rosy pink) and in full leaf. Its dark reddish purple foliage is more colorful in moderate climates. Zones 6 to 9.

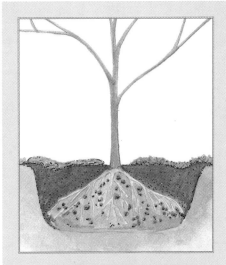

PLANTING A BAREROOT TREE

In mild climates, plant a redbud tree bareroot while dormant in winter; elsewhere plant in fall or very early spring before the buds open.

1 Loosen the soil in the planting site in a circle 3 to 4 feet wide and about 12 inches deep; mound it up slightly in the center.

2 Dig a shallow trench around the outside of the circle, breaking up clods. Use this soil in step 3.

3 Untangle the bare roots. Prune off broken or rotted segments and any severely girdled roots. Set the tree on the mound and spread out the roots. Cover the roots with soil, firming evenly over the top of the mound.

4 Cover the mound and the loosened soil around it with a 3- to 4-inch layer of organic mulch. It will hold the soil in place and conserve moisture.

HINOKI FALSE CYPRESS
Chamaecyparis obtusa

Zones: 5–8

Type: Evergreen

Light: Full sun to part shade

Size: 40–60 ft. tall, 15–30 ft. wide

Form: Narrow pyramid

Growth Rate: Slow to moderate

Interest: Dark green, scale-like needles, lighter underneath; tiny brown cones

Hinoki false cypress foliage is among the most beautiful of its genus. Curving, fan-shaped sprays of needles are borne on flattened stems. Short branches droop slightly at the tips, imparting a graceful appearance especially beautiful under a covering of snow. Most trees in cultivation are named cultivars selected for interesting shapes and needle color. The species rarely grows beyond 50 feet except in its native Japan. Dwarf varieties are grown as shrubs, often in rock gardens.

HOW TO GROW
Hinoki false cypress flourishes in cool-summer climates in moist, well-drained, acidic or neutral soil of average fertility. It does well in hot climates as long as it has ample

humidity and some relief from intense sunlight in both summer and winter. High filtered shade is best. Avoid hot, dry climates and windy sites. Prune out brown patches caused by drying winds. Hose down your tree frequently to wash off dust and supply extra humidity. Plant Hinoki false cypress from containers when possible to avoid root disturbance. Keep the area around newly planted trees well mulched to cool their roots and preserve moisture.

LANDSCAPE USE

The soft outline of Hinoki false cypress makes it one of the best specimen trees for light shade. Planted alone or in groups, it lends a stateliness to formal landscape designs. Use it as a backdrop for shrubs and perennials, or as an accent to broadleaved trees, especially those bearing tinted foliage such as flowering plum, purple beech, and smoke tree.

Hinoki false cypress is used extensively in Japanese-style gardens. Its rich green foliage blends well with other conifers and Japanese maples, contrasting sharply with gray gravel pathways.

Top Choices

- C. 'Crippsii' is a broad tree with dense foliage tinted yellowish gold, mainly at branch ends.

- C. 'Nana Gracilis' develops a pleasing, graceful form. Dark emerald green foliage is closely set on short, compact branches. Very slow growing, it reaches 6 to 10 feet after many years.

Taylor's Tips

PRUNING FALSE CYPRESS

You may find more than one kind of foliage on false cypress. Juvenile leaves are needle-like and prickly while mature leaves are scaly, like those of a mature juniper.

Prune out any branches on false cypress cultivars whose foliage reverts to the juvenile type. On some varieties, such as *C. pisifera* 'Squarrosa', the juvenile foliage persists even on mature trees.

PRIZED SPECIMENS

The numerous and often dramatic cultivars of *C. pisifera* 'Sawara', false cypress, are highly prized despite their slow growth.

- *C. p.* 'Filifera', or threadleaf false cypress, has extremely delicate, thin branchlets that drape like bunches of string. This variety and the similar gold-tinted 'Filifera Aurea' rarely exceed 20 feet.

- *C. p.* 'Plumosa', plume cypress, reaches 20 to 30 feet and is one of the most cold hardy of the species. It also has one of the most interesting textures: Foliage and branches take on the look of billowy, ferny plumes.

FRINGE TREE
Chionanthus virginicus

Zones: 5–9

Type: Deciduous

Light: Full to part sun

Size: 15–30 ft. tall, 15–30 ft. wide

Form: Broad and spreading, open branched

Growth Rate: Slow

Interest: Lustrous green leaves, yellow in autumn; fringed white spring flowers; ½-in., deep blue drupes in summer and fall

Fringe tree is considered by many to be our most magnificent native tree. There is an irresistible appeal to its late-spring canopy filled with bright white, spicily fragrant, dangling panicles of lacy flowers. Bluish purple, ½-inch fruits form in summer on female trees and persist for months. In autumn, the medium to dark green glossy leaves turn yellow in cheerful contrast to the dark fruits. In the garden, fringe tree tends to stay under 20 feet tall.

HOW TO GROW

Fringe tree grows best in moist, slightly acidic, fertile soil, but it doesn't mind wet or dry conditions, wind, or urban pollution. Blossoming is heaviest and fall color richest in full sun, although blooming still occurs in part shade.

Care is minimal. If you plant your tree in a lawn, the fertilizer that you give your grass should be ample for steady tree growth. For trees beyond the lawn area, fertilize only lightly in spring or not at all. If scale is a problem, apply a dormant oil spray in winter.

LANDSCAPE USE

This superb tree would make an ideal specimen in a small garden except for its long dormancy. Since blossoms and leaves appear fairly late in spring, it is better used out of the main spotlight. Include it in or behind a shrub border, beside a patio, or at the end of a terrace. It works well in a raised planter with low perennials or ground covers underneath. Train it as either a single- or multi-stemmed tree, depending on the site. Near a patio or entry, and wherever space is limited, train to a single leader. Encourage a bushy habit in a lawn where there is room to spread, or in a border when using fringe tree for a screen.

ANOTHER FRINGE TREE

Chinese fringe tree, *C. retusus,* is very similar to fringe tree in appearance, but smaller in scale. Flowers smother the canopy in a spectacular dense white fleece. It bears smaller, leathery leaves and blooms a few weeks later in most zones. Gray to brown bark peels off in winter for year-round interest.

When you purchase a Chinese fringe tree, look for the structure that will suit your landscape. Some develop a single trunk and grow 20 to 25 feet with an open-branching structure. Others sold as large shrubs will reach 15 to 20 feet with long branches and a rounded crown.

IT TAKES TWO

Fringe trees bear either male or female flowers on separate trees. Male flowers are showier, since the individual blossoms are larger and the panicles are longer. When you purchase a fringe tree, look for labeling that indicates the gender of the tree you are buying. Fruits form only on female trees that are pollinated, which means that a male tree must be nearby. Birds love these small, dark blue, berrylike drupes.

YELLOWWOOD
Cladrastis lutea

Zones: 3–8

Type: Deciduous

Light: Full sun

Size: 30–50 ft. tall, 40–50 ft. wide

Form: Open, rounded

Growth Rate: Moderate

Interest: Long green leaves, yellow in fall; fragrant white flowers in spring to early summer; beanlike pods in fall and winter

Yellowwood produces a remarkable floral canopy in late spring and early summer, looking very much like white wisteria. As blossoms fade, large yellow-green leaves deepen to bright green, then turn clear yellow in fall. Flattened seedpods hang from branch ends, often persisting into winter. Most yellowwood trees begin flowering when they are ten to twelve years old. They may bloom abundantly only every two or three years.

HOW TO GROW
Like many other deep-rooted trees, yellowwood should be planted in deep, loamy soil when very young. It will not survive in waterlogged conditions, but will withstand long periods of drought. Though yellowwood grows naturally along rivers and streams, it is always found in

fast-draining soil. Yellowwood trees often require corrective pruning to improve their structural strength. Many trees form a narrow crotch that splits easily in high winds. Prune so that branches form a wide crotch, ideally at a 45-degree angle from the trunk. Prune only in summer, since sap pours heavily from cuts made while trees are dormant in winter and spring.

LANDSCAPE USE

Considered by many to be "the perfect tree," yellowwood is undeniably beautiful. When used as a background tree, the abundant blooms from a distance look like skirted ballerinas; up close, they are mildly fragrant. This tree's manageable size makes it a valuable shade tree for both large and small properties. Its shade is light enough and roots deep enough for shade-tolerant plants to grow underneath. The bright green compound leaves are a useful accent against darker green conifers and larger deciduous trees such as hornbeam, maple, and oak. With some protection for its brittle wood against heavy wind, this tree can be long lived, surviving well over a hundred years.

Top Choices

- C. 'Rosea' is a beautiful variety that bears lovely pink flowers.
- C. 'Sweetshade' is a vigorous variety that may resist leafhopper damage.

PROTECTING TREE ROOTS

Severing any roots stresses a tree; cutting those close to the trunk can destroy up to half of the root function. Before you begin any construction projects that involve excavation near your tree, such as trenching for irrigation or drainage lines, set up a protective barrier that will restrict activity to areas outside the root zone.

If it is inevitable that roots will be damaged, remove soil carefully and prune roots rather than ripping them out with construction equipment. If possible, excavate by hand and tunnel under or bridge over roots to protect them.

When you plant a deep-rooted tree such as yellowwood, select the site carefully; moving it after it's established will destroy deep anchoring roots as well as shallow feeder roots.

KOUSA DOGWOOD
Cornus kousa

Zones: 5–8

Type: Deciduous

Light: Full to part sun

Size: To 25 ft. tall, 25 ft. wide

Form: Upright

Growth Rate: Slow to moderate

Interest: Dark green, oval leaves, richly tinted in fall; showy, colorful bracts in spring; fall berries

The spectacular white blossoms of kousa dogwood are reason enough to plant this stately tree. Kousa dogwood has a strong, upright habit with tiers of branches holding dark green leaves. In late summer to fall, round, bumpy red berries hang from the stems and the leaves turn to rich shades of yellow and scarlet. Flowering about three weeks after flowering dogwood, Kousa dogwood extends the fresh, springlike look of the garden almost into summer.

HOW TO GROW
Kousa dogwood grows equally well in full or part sun. Plant in well-drained soil that has been amended with organic matter to help retain soil moisture. Mulch after

planting with bark chips or pine straw. Water during dry periods. Kousa dogwood does not need pruning or other care and is very resistant to pests and diseases, including borers and spot anthracnose.

LANDSCAPE USE

Kousa dogwoods make excellent specimen trees for lawns or other open areas. Their tiered branching and full foliage soften the hard lines of buildings and other structures, while the decorative bark and berries provide interest in winter. Set plants near shrub borders or mass plantings of conifers for gentle contrasts. Planted near perennial borders, kousa dogwoods add a touch of sophistication to almost any garden design.

Top Choices

- C. 'Benji Fuji' bears deep, rose-pink blossoms and leaves marked with red veins.

- C. 'Lustgaren Weeping' has white flowers, red fruit, and weeping branches.

- C. 'Summer Stars' is one of the longest-flowering varieties, with white bracts that linger for over a month after opening in late spring. In fall the deep green leaves turn maroon-purple.

- C. var. *chinensis* 'Milky Way' produces an amazing number of rich white flowers that cling to the branches longer than do most varieties.

MORE DOGWOODS

Kousa and flowering dogwoods aren't the only *Cornus* species worthy of attention. Here are some others that you might find just the thing to fill a niche in your landscape.

Cornelian cherry dogwood, *C. mas*, is vigorous and shrublike but of tree proportions. In spring the branches are covered with masses of tiny yellow blossoms that produce bright red, edible fruits in summer, tasty in syrup and preserves. Cornelian cherry dogwood is free of pests and diseases; it is suited to woodland edges where dark backgrounds set off its showy blooms. 'Golden Glory' reaches 20 feet tall. It has abundant golden yellow blooms in early spring and red, cherrylike fruits in summer. Zones 4 to 8.

Pagoda dogwood, *C. alternifolia*, reaches 20 to 25 feet tall with tiers of attractive gray-barked branches. Flat blossom clusters are scattered over the tops of the branches in mid- to late spring. This hardy species is especially good in the cold, windy conditions of the Midwest. It has reddish purple fall foliage and red-stemmed, dark blue fruits attractive to wildlife. It grows in full sun or full shade. Zones 3 to 7.

FLOWERING DOGWOOD
Cornus florida

Zones: 5–9

Type: Deciduous

Light: Full sun to full shade

Size: To 25 ft. tall, 15–30 ft. wide

Form: Upright, spreading

Growth Rate: Slow to moderate

Interest: Dark green, oval leaves, tinted red in fall; insignificant true flowers but showy bracts in spring; red fall berries

One of the best-loved trees, flowering dogwood is among the loveliest signs of spring. The flowers, with buttonlike centers and colorful white to nearly petal-like red bracts, combine in a captivating display before the leaves unfold. In fall the foliage turns red to maroon and the branches are decorated with shiny red berries. Always deserving of a prominent position for its all-season beauty, flowering dogwood is a favorite not only for a woodland garden, but also for a patio, lawn, or terrace.

HOW TO GROW

Flowering dogwood thrives in part to full shade and can tolerate full sun where water is abundant; it needs part or filtered shade in drier conditions. Longevity depends on fast drainage, unpolluted air, and good air circulation. Trees planted in northern areas should originate from the same climate zone where they are to be grown to guarantee cold hardiness and heavy flowering.

Flowering dogwood is sometimes troubled by borers, insects that tunnel into the trunk. Control pest problems with regular watering and fertilizing. Spot anthracnose, a serious fungal disease that produces brown spots on leaves, can be controlled with mancozeb in spring. Follow the directions on the label.

LANDSCAPE USE

Flowering dogwood adds grace to any garden or yard. Use it as a specimen or mingled with conifers in a shrub border. Placed near an entryway or patio, the flowers and tiered branches add a sophisticated accent to buildings. In woodland settings, there is no finer understory tree. The plants are also good in wildlife gardens and near rock or water gardens.

Top Choices

- C. 'Cherokee Chief' is a very popular variety with deep red bracts and pinkish new growth maturing to green.

- C. 'Cherokee Sunset' bears red bracts on stems lined with green leaves edged in yellow. It is anthracnose resistant.

- C. 'Cloud 9' has abundant, large, snow white bracts on spreading branches.

THE BEST OF BOTH

The most significant new dogwoods to emerge in years are the Stellar hybrids, also known as the Rutgers hybrids (C. x *rutgersensis*). They were developed at Rutgers University by geneticist and plant breeder Dr. Elwin Orton in an effort to maintain the beauty of the flowering and kousa dogwoods while increasing disease and pest resistance. The following varieties have shown high resistance to dogwood borer and good resistance to spot anthracnose, which can be fatal.

- C. 'Aurora' is a handsome tree with a dense habit and white, overlapping bracts. This tree offers excellent fall color.

- C. 'Celestial' grows upright with pure white bracts.

- C. 'Constellation' is a very vigorous grower, bearing white bracts that do not overlap.

- C. 'Ruth Ellen' produces abundant, large white bracts that nearly cover the broad, spreading canopy.

- C. 'Stellar Pink' bears large bracts in a rich shade of pink.

WASHINGTON HAWTHORN
Crataegus phaenopyrum

Zones: 3–8

Type: Deciduous

Light: Full sun

Size: 20–25 ft. tall, 20 ft. wide

Form: Single or multi-trunked, rounded to spreading

Growth Rate: Moderate to fast

Interest: Glossy green leaves, orange-red in fall; white, flat flower clusters; red drupes

The Washington hawthorn is never out of season. In late spring, it is filled with flat clusters of tiny white flowers. Summer interest lies in the maplelike, bright green leaves and developing fruits, which, by autumn, turn glossy orange-red. In winter, they decorate the bare, horizontal branches until the fruits are eaten by birds. Despite its 1- to 3-inch-long, needlelike thorns, this tough, adaptable tree is one of the best hawthorns for home landscapes.

HOW TO GROW
Native to the South and East, this hawthorn species withstands heat and humidity. It is also highly successful in cold-winter and dry-summer climates and in windy sites. Always attractive, it thrives in any type of soil, even

heavy clay with poor drainage. Where rain is frequent in summer, allow space around it for good air circulation. No fertilizer is needed. If you grow Washington hawthorn as a hedge, allow plenty of room for it to spread to avoid the need for heavy trimming. Make pruning cuts only during the growing season. Trees in any location may need their thorny lower limbs removed altogether if they protrude dangerously.

LANDSCAPE USE

Washington hawthorn should be kept away from high-traffic walkways and children's play areas. The thorns may be useful, however, if you grow this tree as a barrier hedge. Use it along a fencerow or driveway rather than near a sidewalk or path. This tree is equally at home in a naturalized setting where wildlife is abundant (deer leave it alone) or in a more formal environment, and it is a good survivor in urban conditions. Its all-season splendor radiates in front of a darker, evergreen background. If cedar-apple rust is a problem in your area, avoid locating it near junipers, cedars, or cypresses; hawthorn can act as an alternate host for this disease.

Top Choices

- C. 'Presidential' is tall (up to 28 feet and almost as wide) and resistant to diseases.

Taylor's Tips

SLOWING THE BLIGHT

Hawthorn is susceptible to fire blight, a bacterium that damages new growth in spring. Recognize it by black, peeling bark and sunken cankers on branches. Damaged branch tips curve into the shape of a shepherd's crook.

To slow the spread of this disease, remove diseased tissue well below the infected area. Make cuts using pruners rinsed in a mild bleach solution before each cut. Destroy the diseased prunings. Washington hawthorn is less susceptible to fire blight than other hawthorn species.

DISEASE-RESISTANT 'WINTER KING'

C. viridis 'Winter King' rivals Washington hawthorn as the best of the genus for ornamental use. It has fewer thorns, is rust resistant, bears larger fruits, and reveals distinctive silvery bark in winter. Its orange-red fruits assume a deeper red in cold winters. Fall color runs to blends of yellows and reds with rich purple highlights.

Plant 'Winter King', which grows to 30 to 40 feet high and wide, only where its lower branches have room to expand, and where nothing grows underneath except early-spring bulbs.

EUROPEAN BEECH
Fagus sylvatica

Zones: 5–8

Type: Deciduous

Light: Full sun

Size: 50–60 ft. tall, 35–45 ft. wide

Form: Broadly dome shaped

Growth Rate: Slow to moderate

Interest: Lustrous, dark green, oval leaves; insignificant flowers; prickly-husked, small nuts

Few shade trees are as awe inspiring as a mature European beech with its lustrous, wavy-edged leaves covering branches that sweep the ground in a wide circle. Like other beech trees, its aspect changes with the seasons. Young leaves, aglow in pale green, open in late spring from long, tapering buds. Summer color is bright green; in autumn, the leaves turn warm golden yellow and rusty brown, holding on for several months. Winter reveals visually textured yet smooth gray bark, often compared with elephant hide.

HOW TO GROW
Plant European beech in full sun in slightly acidic soil that has good drainage. The species and varieties require a constant supply of air in the root zone, which means that they will not survive in heavy, wet, or compacted

soil. Restrict all activity to several yards beyond the drip line. If you remove any branches or clip European beech, make cuts only in summer to avoid bleeding. This tree is usually trouble-free except in very hot climates, where it struggles and foliage burns.

LANDSCAPE USE

Wherever you plant stately European beech, be sure it has room to spread unencumbered. This tree can be sheared and grown quite attractively as a hedge, but cutting back side branches on a specimen tree ruins its shape. Roots are shallow and protrude above the soil line.

Top Choices

- *F.* 'Pendula', weeping beech, has an irregular, spreading form with branches that flow to the ground from one or several trunks. Some are quite tall and fountain-like in habit; others drape tentlike and, with age, can become far wider than they are tall.

- *F.* 'Tricolor', also known as 'Roseomarginata', is the best beech for small gardens; it can be grown in a container. It is slow growing—usually no more than 25 feet tall. The name refers to its exquisitely colored leaves. Green-centered leaves—purple on 'Purpurea Tricolor'—are rimmed with pink and cream margins. This tree must have an environment with half shade to protect it from sunburn. In shade, it is less dense and more open branched.

A GRAND SPECIMEN

Suited for estates and properties with broad sweeps of lawn, European beech is too large for most home landscapes—with the exception of the smaller-sized cultivars. Where space permits, this is one of the very best trees and one deserving of highest prominence. To view it fairly, set it so its spreading branches can be seen unobscured.

Withhold pruning, unless there are damaged branches, so the lower limbs bend to the ground. There is nothing like a photo with a great beech as a backdrop, dwarfing the people standing in front. European beech grows fairly slowly; if you plant one now, it won't be full sized until the next generation takes the pictures.

PLANTING CARE

At planting time, give European beech a little extra care. Dig the hole several feet wide and spread out the roots to promote their shallow, horizontal habit. Cut back any long roots to encourage branching. Keep the top of the rootball level with the existing grade and free of additional soil. Cover the planting area with a very shallow layer of mulch.

FRANKLIN TREE

Franklinia alatamaha

Zones: 5–8

Type: Deciduous

Light: Full to part sun

Size: 10–20 ft. tall, 6–12 ft. wide

Form: Single or multi-stemmed, rounded

Growth Rate: Moderate

Interest: Glossy, dark green leaves; good fall color; cupped, 3-in. white flowers in late summer and fall; nutlike, woody fruits in fall

The Franklin tree, named after Benjamin Franklin, is a jewel of a tree. It never exceeds 30 feet tall, making it perfect for small gardens. In late summer and early autumn, it bears lovely white blossoms similar to camellias. Flowering continues as leaves turn brilliant orange and scarlet. In winter, smooth bark and silky young branchlets are most prominent when Franklin tree is grown with several slender trunks.

HOW TO GROW

Franklin tree requires moist and loose, well-drained soil for its small root mass. Fortify the soil with compost or other organic matter to improve drainage. In heavy, wet soil, roots are highly susceptible to fungal disease. For best drainage, plant on a slightly elevated, circular mound. Acidic conditions are best, but slight alkalinity is tolerable. Don't fertilize at planting time, and never use a water-soluble chemical product, which may burn sensitive roots. In spring of the second year, mix well-aged manure or a slow-release, granular fertilizer into a 3- to 4-inch layer of organic mulch and spread it over the root zone. Pruning is rarely necessary. If you prune to shape, make cuts in fall or winter.

LANDSCAPE USE

Franklin tree is a good choice for a single tree for a patio or courtyard, a specimen on a terrace, or a filler in a restricted space. It is also highly ornamental featured in a lawn (with adequate drainage). In a shrub border, Franklin tree's late flowering is a valuable attribute. When set among shrubs, the bare trunks with pale, striped bark are hidden; they are more visible in winter when Franklin tree stands alone. It presents a nice foil for out-of-bloom azaleas and rhododendrons in either the open landscape or a shaded woodland, though you will sacrifice some of the Franklin tree's flowers in shade.

In the South, grow Franklin tree in a container or planter box filled with a purchased, sterile mix for the best results. Don't contaminate the sterile planting medium by adding garden soil. Soils in the South appear to harbor a disease organism fatal to this tree. It is important to use a light mix that will ensure fast drainage. In the Pacific Northwest a different problem arises. There, gardeners may be disappointed with sparse blooms in rainy fall weather.

STARTING SMALL

All trees and shrubs grow best and fastest when they are planted very young. For Franklin tree, planting young is a matter of its very survival. Since its sparse root system is easily damaged, you lessen the risk of injury by planting it young.

You may actually have the most success if you start Franklin tree from seeds. Harvest seeds as soon as they are ripe in mid-to late fall; you'll find several inside each woody fruit. It is critical that the seeds do not dry out. Plant them immediately, or try refrigerating first for a month in moist sand and then planting them. Your tree will bloom in six to seven years.

GINKGO
Ginkgo biloba

Zones: 4–9

Type: Deciduous

Light: Full sun

Size: 50–80 ft. tall, 30–40 ft. wide

Form: Columnar to pyramidal, then wide spreading

Growth Rate: Moderate

Interest: Green, fan-shaped leaves, yellow in autumn; insignificant flowers; fleshy fruits on female trees

Ginkgo's wavy, pale green, fan-shaped leaves resemble those of the maidenhair fern. Ginkgo puts on its best show in autumn, when its pale green leaves turn soft yellow. The canopy is set wondrously aglow when backlit by afternoon sun. Its pale beige to gray bark shows contrasting vertical marks. Cultivated varieties are either male or female. Be sure to buy a male tree. Females produce fruits whose fleshy seed covering is malodorous when crushed and causes a litter problem on paving.

HOW TO GROW
Plant ginkgo in full sun in ordinary garden conditions. Growth will be slow in poor soil, and moderate to fast in deep loam soil or with supplemental fertilizing. Until your tree is well established, keep the soil reasonably

moist, but not wet. Later on, cut back on watering. Ginkgo withstands some drought as it matures, but growth may be slower.

Seed-grown trees may develop more than one central leader. Prune to shape and to balance branches. Many young trees may be more gawky than graceful; with maturity, they improve in shape without pruning.

LANDSCAPE USE

A group planting of ginkgo trees highlights the clouds of yellow foliage in fall and the handsome, ridged bark in winter. Very adaptable and tolerant of salt and pollution, this is a good tree for cities. The graceful spreading canopy supplies pools of shade around a residence and along the street. It is best to plant a named cultivar with a compact form wherever space is limited; mature species trees can spread widely.

Top Choices

Select the following male gingko cultivars for their branching habit and leaf color.

- G. 'Autumn Gold' is very regularly shaped and offers possibly the best of any golden fall color.

- G. 'Mayfield' is narrow and upright, growing up to 60 feet tall but only 25 feet wide.

- G. 'Saratoga', a male clone, develops a strong central trunk and compact habit. It grows about 40 feet tall and 25 feet wide.

- G. 'Princeton Sentry' is narrowly pyramidal and a good choice for a street tree.

A LIVING FOSSIL

One of the most impressive fall-colored trees, ginkgo brings grace and elegance to modern landscapes. Yet this is the most ancient of broadleafed trees.

Ginkgo's appearance continues unchanged from fossil records that date back over 150 million years. Like its relatives, redwood and sequoia, ginkgo can live to an astonishing age—more than a thousand years. Interest in this tree peaked in the twentieth century.

MORE THAN GOOD LOOKS

In Asia, the inner nutlike gingko seeds are roasted and eaten as a delicacy, though the juice from the smelly fruits is considered toxic. An extract from the leaves is used as a circulatory stimulant in herbal medicine and as a treatment for Alzheimer's disease.

KENTUCKY COFFEE TREE
Gymnocladus dioica

Zones: 4–8

Type: Deciduous

Light: Full sun

Size: 60–70 ft. tall, 40–50 ft. wide

Form: Narrow, open, oval crown

Growth Rate: Slow to moderate

Interest: Dark blue-green, compound leaves with many small leaflets; greenish white flowers in late spring; beanlike pods in fall and winter

This is a resilient shade tree, adapted to many conditions. It bears compound leaves made up of many small leaflets. They unfold, pink tinted, in late spring, remain dark blue-green through summer, and turn yellow in fall. Greenish white flower panicles open after the leaves bud out. Long, plump, reddish brown seedpods form on female trees and persist throughout winter. The attractive brown bark is rough textured with furrowed ridges and scales.

HOW TO GROW
Kentucky coffee tree can grow with no additional care after it is established, though it looks better with a little maintenance. For fastest growth, plant it in full sun and

deep, rich soil, either acidic or alkaline. If your soil is very poor and growth slows, fertilize lightly after the second year. Female trees drop seedpods in spring; after leaf loss, both male and female trees drop long rachises—the stems that hold individual leaflets. Bagging everything with a lawn mower is a fast way to clean up the mess.

LANDSCAPE USE

Kentucky coffee tree is handsome and trouble-free through heat and cold, heavy soil, and drought. Essentially pest- and disease-free, it seems unfazed by urban pollution, salt, or wind. This is one of the best trees for creating high, filtered shade. Its divided leaves offer an airy openness, allowing lawn and other plants to flourish beneath. Sparse but picturesque branches angle upward and stay fairly bare, with foliage heaviest at the ends. It is difficult to predict the mature shape of seed-grown trees, but most are narrow for many years, then develop a broad canopy.

CAUTION: *Although early settlers roasted beans from Kentucky coffee tree, research has shown that the seeds and leaves are carcinogenic. The sticky pulp surrounding the seeds contains an alkaloid that is also harmful. Since it can cause surface damage to vehicles parked underneath, plant only male trees along the street or paved walkways.*

Top Choice

- G. 'Espresso' produces no seeds. While somewhat hard to find, it is worth seeking out if you want to reduce cleanup chores.

REMOVING A BRANCH

Kentucky coffee tree needs no routine pruning, but if a branch breaks it will need pruning to help it heal. A clean cut assists in a natural process called compartmentalization, which seals off an injured area with a decay-resistant wall.

Look for the collar—the bulge where the damaged branch joins the trunk (or another branch)—and cut just outside it, without cutting the collar. The tree will produce a protective growth that seals off the wound. Never use a wound dressing, which can actually harm the tree by promoting the growth of decay organisms.

On most trees, make pruning cuts in winter or early spring before buds begin to swell. At this time, the tree has the greatest reserves for new growth.

CAROLINA SILVERBELL

Halesia carolina

Zones: 4–8

Type: Deciduous

Light: Full to part sun

Size: 30–50 ft. tall, 20–30 ft. wide

Form: Irregular, rounded, low branched

Growth Rate: Moderate to fast

Interest: Yellow-green, oval leaves; white, bell-shaped flowers; winged, 1- to 2-in. seedpods

Carolina silverbell, or snowdrop tree, is named for the profusion of dainty, white, bell-like blooms that open just as the leaves begin to appear and dangle in showy clusters under the branches for about two weeks. Brown, winged seedpods flutter attractively beneath yellow foliage in fall. This is a captivating small tree with thin, smooth leaves, and graceful, arching branches that rise close to the ground and grow to a rounded canopy. The overall effect is light and open.

How to Grow

Like other plants native to woodlands, Carolina silverbell needs deep soil that is humus rich, well drained, and acidic to neutral pH. In alkaline, salty, or compacted soil, the leaves develop chlorotic yellow spots and growth slows. Keep roots cool under a layer of organic mulch; Carolina silverbell does not thrive in hot-summer and mild-winter climates. If rains are infrequent, water to keep the soil moist. In well-drained soil, it is completely resistant to pests and diseases.

Usually sold with several stems, Carolina silverbell will grow as a multi-trunked tree unless it is trained to a central leader. Let your planting site determine which shape is best. Protect it from strong winds and don't move it after planting.

LANDSCAPE USE

Carolina silverbell makes an excellent tree for a patio, where you can look up at the pendant blossoms. It is also pretty in the corner of a lawn, where the white bells stand out against a background of dark evergreens. Native to lightly shaded woodlands, it does well with shrubs, thriving among rhododendrons, azaleas, and other acid-loving plants. Under-plant with tall red and yellow tulips combined with ferns, foamflowers, par-tridgeberries, or creeping lilyturfs.

Top Choice

- *H. monticola,* mountain silverbell, is similar to Carolina silverbell in every way except that it grows taller and has larger leaves, flowers, and seedpods. 'Rosea' has pink flowers.

FROM SHRUB TO TREE

Many plants with multiple stems can grow as either large shrubs or small trees. (See *Amelanchier, Arbutus, Cercis, Magnolia.*) For a tree form, designate one or more stems as trunks and eliminate the rest. Prune in late winter or early spring while the tree is dormant.

1 Remove branches at their base just outside the collar (see page 55, "Removing a Branch"). Where branches fork at a crotch, cut near the top of the ridge of bark that forms in the center of the crotch, angling out-ward so the cut ends opposite the bottom of the collar. For small cuts, use bypass shears or loppers; for larger cuts, use a pruning saw.

2 Give the tree a year to recover after planting before you remove the lower side branches.

GOLDEN-RAIN TREE
Koelreuteria paniculata

Zones: 5–9

Type: Deciduous

Light: Full sun

Size: 30–40 ft. tall, 20–40 ft. wide

Form: Irregular to rounded and spreading

Growth Rate: Moderate to fast

Interest: Compound leaf with lobed leaflets; yellow flowers in summer; brownish red seedpods

Long panicles of tiny flowers as bright as goldenrod cover golden-rain tree in early to midsummer. Spent blossoms shatter and drop to the ground in a "golden rain" of petals. In fall, puffed, papery seedpods that look like miniature Chinese lanterns contrast with the dark green foliage. The fruits are first lime green, then beige before they mature to a reddish brown. In spring, color derives from the young, unfolding leaves, coral-pink with bronze or purple hues.

HOW TO GROW
Golden-rain prospers in wind and drought, warm and cold climates, and infertile or rich soil, either acidic or alkaline. Plant it bareroot, balled-and-burlapped, or from a container. Give it ample water until established;

afterward, water only during dry periods. If soil is poor and growth is slow, fertilize lightly. Too much fertilizer promotes fast growth and weak wood. As the tree grows, you may need to thin the canopy if shade becomes too dense. Start with a good branching pattern. A single trunk is best on a street tree; multiple stems make a nice architectural statement in a lawn.

LANDSCAPE USE

Golden-rain possesses unusual versatility for a flowering tree. A good choice for cities, it can withstand the stress of root restriction and poor drainage in compacted soil, alkalinity from paving and salt runoff, and air pollution and reflected heat along streets. It is an ideal tree in a landscape, offering protective summer shade and allowing warming winter sun to filter through when planted next to a residence. In the garden, its deep roots don't interfere with shrubs, bulbs, annuals, or perennials planted underneath.

Top Choices

- *K. bipinnata,* Chinese flame tree, bears longer leaves and is otherwise similar.

- *K.* 'September' is similar to the species but blooms about five weeks later (hence the name).

ESTABLISHING A TREE

Getting a tree established often involves lengthy follow-up care. For golden-rain tree, care must extend over a two-year period before growth is fast and vigorous. Keep the soil mulched and evenly moist—not wet—throughout the growing season. If necessary, erect a wind shield. In addition:

- At planting time, avoid fertilizing, which causes rapid, weak growth. Do not amend the soil, because this inhibits root expansion. Fertilize in the second or third year only if growth is slow, ideally by mulching with compost or chopped leaves.

- For strongest trunks, avoid staking if the tree will stand alone. Never use only one stake, set stakes too close to the tree, or leave them in place too long. (See page 31, "Staking a Tree.")

- Avoid pruning a young tree; removing foliage reduces its capacity to produce food needed for normal growth and vigor. Once the tree is established, prune only as needed.

CRAPE MYRTLE
Lagerstroemia indica

Zones: 7–9

Type: Deciduous

Light: Full sun

Size: 15–25 ft. tall, 8–10 ft. wide

Form: Vase shaped to rounded

Growth Rate: Fast

Interest: Oval leaves with good fall color; summer flowers; seedpods and attractive bark in winter

Few plants can rival crape myrtle's spectacular midsummer bloom. This modest-sized tree outdoes itself with a long and brilliant floral display in shades of red, rose, pink, purple, or white. Small, crepe-papery flowers compose 6- to 8-inch-long panicles at the tip of each branch. As blossoms fade, leaves turn from dark green to coppery orange, yellow, and red. In winter, crape myrtle's thin bark peels off, exposing irregular blotches of pinkish brown that give the smooth, slender branches a dappled look.

HOW TO GROW

Easy to grow, crape myrtle is a favorite in the hot South and West. In colder climates, it is often treated like a perennial and cut to the ground each spring, blooming on new branches. It does best in fast-draining soil with water-retentive organic matter. Water deeply to encourage deep rooting, which makes plants drought resistant. On tree forms, remove low branches and basal suckers as they appear. To increase blossoming points, cut back branches 1 to 1½ feet during dormancy. Reducing irrigation in late summer may help intensify autumn leaf color. Look for hybrids that are resistant to powdery mildew, which afflicts many crape myrtles, especially in damp, cool climates.

LANDSCAPE USE

This is a sun lover, ideal for the reflected heat of a street or roadway. Its small size fits easily under utility wires. For a spectacular background for late-summer outdoor activities, plant several along a driveway, in front of a fence, or at the edge of a lawn. At the back of a border, trees in flower fill in above the summer greenery of shrubs and out-of-bloom perennials. Hues can be intense, so use the same color or variety when you plant crape myrtle in groups.

Top Choices

- *L.* 'Natchez' has especially attractive bark and large, white flowers over a long period. It resists pests and diseases.

- *L.* 'Sioux' also offers good pest and disease resistance, plus intense pink flowers, on 15-foot plants.

- *L.* 'Zuni' grows to 9 feet and has long-lasting, rosy lilac blooms. It is also disease resistant.

A CONTAINER GARDEN

Crape myrtle makes a great container plant. Grow it in pots or in planter boxes with a low ground cover for year-round enjoyment. Give trees winter protection in very cold climates, then move them into view during their growing season or bloom period.

1 Select a container large enough to hold the mature rootball. Crape myrtle will grow quickly.

2 Use a soil-less potting mix with organic material, sand, and vermiculite that drains quickly but will hold moisture.

3 Fertilize during the growing season with a slow-release product, following package directions.

4 Every two years, lift out the rootball, trim any wrapped roots, and add new potting mix.

SWEET GUM
Liquidambar styraciflua

Zones: 6–9

Type: Deciduous

Light: Full sun

Size: 60–70 ft. tall, 20–40 ft. wide

Form: Pyramidal to rounded

Growth Rate: Moderate to fast

Interest: Star-shaped leaves with bright fall color; prickly seed balls

Sweet gum is prized for its flamboyant fall foliage in shades of orange, golden yellow, and burgundy. In mild-winter climates, where seasonal changes are scarcely noticed, this tree is one of the few that provide reliable fall color. Leaf color varies widely from tree to tree, and it also fluctuates year to year.

How to Grow

Plant sweet gum where its shallow roots will not raise pavement or interfere with other plants. It will tolerate poor drainage and dry soil, though not long periods of drought. Growth is usually slow for the first year or two after transplanting, and more rapid after the tree is established. Sweet gum prefers slightly acidic soil. If your soil is alkaline, expect some yellowing from chlorosis.

Sweet gum naturally retains branches low on the trunk. Leave them in place to shade the bark and to invest your tree with its own character. No pruning is needed, except for damaged or deadwood. Never remove or cut back the central leader.

LANDSCAPE USE

Choose a location that will take advantage of sweet gum's best qualities—shade and autumn color—while minimizing its shortcomings—shallow rooting and litter from seed balls. Species trees, which tend to be broader spreading, may offer the most shade. Some named varieties, such as 'Festival' and 'Kia', are more columnar and practical in narrow spaces. In winter, the seed balls are quite attractive as they hang among the bare, fissured branches. They are a drawback when sweet gum is planted near paving; they must be swept up in parking and traffic areas and raked off a lawn.

Top Choices

- *L.* 'Burgundy' has been selected for excellent dark red to purple fall color. It holds its leaves into the winter.

- *L.* 'Gold Dust' (also known as 'Aurea' and 'Variegata') bears variously tinted leaves, some gold flecked, some green, and others gold. Fall color is pink and burgundy.

- *L.* 'Moraine' is one of the fastest-growing sweet gums, exceptionally cold hardy and flaming red in autumn.

- *L.* 'Palo Alto' has good orange-red color in fall, even in mild climates.

DEALING WITH SHALLOW ROOTS

Under a shallow-rooted tree such as sweet gum, the roots beat out the grass for water and nutrients, leaving you with thin, unattractive turf that easily becomes weed infested. Further, when roots protrude above ground, they can be damaged by mowing and in turn endanger the health of the tree. Planting ground covers and flowering plants is equally frustrating. There just isn't enough soil or moisture.

The best defense is to yield control to the roots and remove the lawn. Using a lawn edging tool or a sharp spade, cut a smooth edge on the turf and cover the soil with 2 to 4 inches of a coarse mulch. A thicker layer inhibits air circulation; a thinner layer allows weeds to grow. Use chipped bark, pine needles, or other organic material.

DECIDUOUS MAGNOLIAS
Magnolia

Zones: 5–9

Type: Deciduous

Light: Full sun to light shade

Size: 10–30 ft. tall, 15–30 ft. wide

Form: Spreading to rounded

Growth Rate: Moderate

Interest: Dark green, oval to oblong leaves; thick, saucer- or star-shaped blossoms in spring

Deciduous magnolias are a group of hardy, mostly shrublike plants that can be left multi-stemmed or trained as single-trunked trees. Though they are winter hardy, flowering occurs so early in spring that blossoms are occasionally nipped when frosts follow a warm spell. Still, the magnificent clouds of color are worth the risk. Trees are handsome in winter with smooth gray bark and attractive branching patterns set off by long, tapering buds.

How to Grow
Plant young trees before bloom in early spring in a permanent location; they are easily shocked when moved and slow to recover after transplanting. Give them deep, humus-rich, acidic soil and regular water. Blossoming is heaviest in full sun, but some shade is tolerable. Keep

them out of heavy winds. Apply a layer of mulch around the root zone after planting and renew annually. Many magnolias get leaf spot late in the season. It blemishes the leaves but does no serious damage.

LANDSCAPE USE

Deciduous magnolias are the consummate small specimen trees. Placed in a lawn or near the edge of a border, they add beauty without overpowering the landscape. For large properties, a group planting is stunning, especially when different types are interplanted together.

Top Choices

- M. x *soulangiana,* saucer magnolia, is a broad-spreading tree and flowers young. 'Alexandrina' has white blooms suffused with purplish pink; 'Lennei' has dark magenta flowers that bloom late enough to miss the frost most years. 'San Jose', another vigorous, rosy purple bloomer, is suited to mild climates, since it is the earliest blooming of the species.

- M. *stellata,* star magnolia, has fragrant, white, 3-inch blossoms that completely cover the 10- to 15-foot shrubs in late winter in mild climates, in midspring elsewhere. 'Royal Star'—one of the very best—has exceptionally large white flowers on a vigorous, shrublike tree. 'Waterlily' has pink buds that open white with pink on the backsides of the petals. Zones 4 to 8.

HYBRID MAGNOLIAS

Perhaps the finest of all the magnolias are the Loebner hybrids, M. x *loebneri.* Similar to the star magnolias, they produce large, showy, fragrant blossoms. Zones 4 to 8.

- M. x *l.* 'Ballerina' reaches 15 to 20 feet tall and bears nicely fragrant blossoms with a blush of pink in the center washing to pure white at the edges.

- M. x *l.* 'Merrill' is a vigorous grower to 35 feet tall with masses of fragrant blossoms that begin as pink buds and open to white. Hardier than most magnolias. Zones 4 to 8.

- M. x *l.* 'Leonard Messel' is a vision in full flower. It reaches 15 to 20 feet tall and bears purplish pink buds that unfurl into 6-inch blossoms of pink-tinted, wavy petals.

A YELLOW MAGNOLIA

M. 'Elizabeth' is a late-flowering, pyramidal magnolia with horizontal branching. Its wonderfully scented blossoms of exquisite beauty are creamy yellow, an unusual color for a magnolia. It is slowly becoming more widely available.

SOUTHERN MAGNOLIA
Magnolia grandiflora

Zones: 7–9

Type: Evergreen

Light: Full to part sun

Size: 60–80 ft. tall, 30–40 ft. wide

Form: Pyramidal to columnar to rounded

Growth Rate: Slow to moderate

Interest: Dark green, oblong leaves; huge, fragrant white flowers in early summer; conelike fruits in fall

For many, the stately southern magnolia reigns alone among the evergreens. It is a grand specimen with glossy leaves, a dark, dense canopy, and immense (6- to 10-inch) white blossoms. Large buds open into cup-shaped, heavily scented flowers. The pure white, sometimes creamy petals surround a prominent yellow center, and darken to a buff color as they fade. Fruits split open when ripe in fall, revealing red seeds.

Most trees are considerably taller than they are wide. Large, dark green, leathery leaves are a downy-textured russet underneath. Though evergreen, southern magnolia continuously drops and replaces its leaves, usually a few each day. For those who love this magnolia, the litter is only a minor nuisance compared to the delights of the profuse, lemon-scented blossoms.

HOW TO GROW

Southern magnolia differs from its deciduous relatives in several ways. It is easy to move once established; it will grow in dry desert heat, but not in cold climates; and its tall trunk makes it a valuable as shade tree. Plant in acidic soil. It needs plentiful water and mulch. In dry winter sun and winds, the leaves brown at the edges.

LANDSCAPE USE

The majestic size of the southern magnolia is both a strength and a limitation in the landscape. As a specimen, it is one of the most impressive broad-leafed trees, and one that needs room to grow. It needs space all around to allow sun to filter through the canopy and to grant its aristocratic bearing full expression. The size of this tree endows it with the noble stature it enjoys in southern gardens.

Top Choices

- *M.* 'Majestic Beauty' produces everything in majestic proportions—immense flowers, large leaves, and a beautiful pyramidal shape to 50 feet tall.

- *M.* 'Stalwart' performs aptly for its name, growing vigorously into a densely crowned tree. This variety also begins flowering at an early age.

COMPACT CULTIVARS

Thanks to nurserymen and their dedication to the beauty of this genus, several smaller—some could be called dwarf—cultivars make it possible to grow this lovely tree in gardens with limited space. Here are some of the best:

- *M.* 'Edith Bogue' is slow to flower and has narrow leaves on trees that grow 30 to 35 feet tall and 15 feet wide. It is hardy in Zone 6 and in protected sites in Zone 5.

- *M.* 'Little Gem' is a shrubby tree at just 15 to 20 feet tall and only 10 feet wide. It blooms young with blossoms 3 to 5 inches across. Zones 8 to 9.

- *M.* 'St. Mary' (also called 'Glen St. Mary') stays low and narrow for many years, reaching about 20 feet tall. Blossoming begins while the tree is young, producing an abundance of 5-inch-wide flowers.

- *M.* 'Samuel Sommer' grows 30 to 40 feet tall and 20 feet wide with rapid vertical growth. Huge flowers are 10 to 14 inches across. Zones 8 to 9.

- *M.* 'Victoria' is a good choice for the Pacific Northwest. It has large flowers (8 to 10 inches) and grows 20 feet tall and 15 feet wide. Zones 6 to 9.

FLOWERING CRAB APPLE
Malus spp.

Zones: 4–9

Type: Deciduous

Light: Full sun

Size: 15–25 ft. tall, 15–25 ft. wide

Form: Vase shaped to rounded or pendulous

Growth Rate: Moderate to fast

Interest: Green or purple leaves; abundant spring flowers; small fruits in red, orange, or yellow from summer into winter

Flowering crab apple is well loved for its delicate appearance and profusion of spring blossoms in white, pink, and rosy red. Forms range from weeping or nearly columnar to those that look much like standard apple trees. Some bear fruits that are large and tasty while the fruits of others are inedible. Trees that bear richly colored fruits attract wildlife, and the tiny apples decorate the bare branches in winter (unless eaten by birds).

HOW TO GROW

Crab apple is most vigorous from Zone 6 north. Plants do best in well-drained, slightly acidic loam, though they tolerate clay and wet soils, too. Plant in full sun for the best flower and fruit displays. Prune a young tree so it develops strong structural branches, removing crossing branches and suckers from the base in late winter or early spring when the tree is dormant. Fertilize lightly, keeping nitrogen to a minimum to balance foliage and flower production. Water during periods of drought. To avoid pest and disease problems, choose resistant varieties.

LANDSCAPE USE

Use crab apple as a colorful accent, or plant a small grove to use as a seasonal screen. Grow varieties that blossom at different times to lengthen the flowering and fruiting seasons. Set narrow trees 15 feet apart, broader-spreading ones 25 feet. They can be espaliered along a sunny wall or fence.

Top Choices

- M. 'Coralburst' has a dense, rounded canopy of foliage and horizontal branching on a tree that grows 15 feet tall and wide. Double, rose flowers bloom from coral-pink buds. It bears a light crop of reddish orange fruits.

- M. 'Donald Wyman' has white flowers that bloom from pinkish red buds. Fruits are glossy bright red throughout winter. The tree has a spreading habit and good resistance to diseases. It grows 20 feet tall and 20 to 25 feet wide.

- M. 'Molten Lava' has a weeping shape and grows 15 feet tall and wide. Deep red buds open into white blossoms. The fruits are glossy orange-red. Foliage turns yellow in fall, and the bark is yellow in winter.

DISEASE-RESISTANT CRAB APPLES

You don't have to sacrifice beauty to have a disease-resistant crab apple tree. There are many varieties, with flower and fruit colors ranging from white to gold to red.

- M. 'Adams' has rose-red buds and flowers that fade to pink. The fruits are red and hold their color. It grows 20 feet tall and 25 feet wide.

- M. 'Harvest Gold' is a narrow, upright variety good for smaller spaces. Its white flowers appear slightly later than most crab apples. Tiny, amber yellow fruits persist into winter.

- M. 'Professor Sprenger' has white flowers and bears reddish orange fruits, persisting into winter. It grows to 25 feet tall and wide, assuming a round shape.

- M. 'Prairiefire' has purplish red flowers from crimson buds on a tree that grows 20 feet tall and 20 feet wide. Fruits are small, shiny, and purplish red.

- M. 'Sugar Tyme' is an upright, 20-foot tree with an oval shape and vigorous growth. Pale pink buds open into white, fragrant flowers. Its heavy crop of red fruits holds through winter unless eaten by birds.

DAWN REDWOOD

Metasequoia glyptostroboides

Zones: 5–9

Type: Deciduous

Light: Full sun

Size: 80–100 ft. tall (estimated), 25–40 ft. wide

Form: Pyramidal

Growth Rate: Fast

Interest: Soft green needles, copper in fall; small brown cones

The dawn redwood, a dinosaur-age conifer that loses its needles in winter, is widely grown in cold climates where coastal redwoods can't survive. Feathery sprays of pale spring growth darken to deep green by summer. Before needles drop in late autumn, the tree becomes a tower of yellow-orange, gold, and copper-bronze. Winter reveals reddish brown inner bark as the outer, darker surface peels in narrow strips. With age, the base broadens, developing buttresslike extensions.

HOW TO GROW

In the right location, dawn redwood reaches tremendous size. A long growing season favors fast growth and seasonal changes. It does best in humus-rich soil and in moist areas with good drainage, but will adapt to drier locations with some irrigation. It will fail in deserts, drying winter winds, or coastal salt spray, and it will burn from reflected heat. Choose a planting site where cold air can drain away in winter. Young growing tips are damaged by frost, so withhold fertilizers after midsummer. (Fertilizers are needed only in very poor soil.) Since extensive growing of dawn redwood started in the 1940s, its ultimate size and performance in cultivation are as yet unknown, so the size in the box at left is an estimate.

LANDSCAPE USE

This is a large tree that needs a spacious site to show off its salient features. It will not shine in a crowded planting, since its graceful outline can be appreciated only from a distance. Plant a single specimen in a lawn or several in a grove. You can also plant dawn redwood in the garden. Its shade is not dense, and broad-spreading trees limbed up will accommodate shade-tolerant plants beneath.

Top Choices

- M. 'National' is a narrow variety with branches that curve strongly upward. Its tall, conelike shape makes a useful vertical at a lakeside, pond, or stream.

- M. 'Sheridan Spire' is even narrower and is more compact than the species.

PREVENTING SOIL COMPACTION

Gardening under trees with foliage or flowering shrubs and perennials introduces root competition that some trees cannot tolerate. Luckily, a young dawn redwood does not seem to mind rivalry in its root zone, but it can't tolerate activity so heavy that the soil becomes compacted.

To protect roots of dawn redwood and other trees from soil compaction, avoid activity in the root zone when the ground is wet. Just walking on a wet surface impedes drainage and forces out air essential for healthy roots. Stay off wet lawns, avoid parking under trees, and don't change the grade or pave over the roots.

COMPANION PLANTS

Plants that do well under dawn redwood are hellebores, astilbes, variegated irises, and ornamental grasses. Cluster low-growing plants around vase-shaped *Stachyurus praecox*, a deciduous shrub (Zones 7 to 9) whose long, pendulous flower stems are showy throughout winter and early spring. Its shiny mahogany branches and fall foliage are echoed in dawn redwood's richly colored, deciduous needles.

SOUR GUM
Nyssa sylvatica

Zones: 3–9

Type: Deciduous

Light: Full or part sun

Size: 30–60 ft. tall, 20–30 ft. wide

Form: Pyramidal, maturing to oblong and rounded

Growth Rate: Slow to moderate

Interest: Shiny green leaves, brightly colored in fall; insignificant flowers; blue-black berries in fall

For outstanding color, you'll find none better than the yellows, deep apricots, hot oranges, crimson reds, and purples that sour gum paints each autumn. Individual leaves are glossy green by late spring. The narrow canopy casts moderate shade, good for use in a lawn. After leaf drop, the mostly horizontal and twisted branches and the rough, blotchy bark are exposed for a picturesque winter silhouette. Birds and other wildlife enjoy the dark, sour fruits that look like olives.

HOW TO GROW
Plant sour gum while it is very young so it becomes established before its strong taproot develops. Older trees may take years to recover from transplanting.

Well-drained, moist, rich loam is best and promotes fastest growth for this otherwise slow grower. However, sour gum tolerates both dry and wet clay soils, a wide pH range, and low fertility. If your tree shows little sign of growth after the second year, apply a balanced fertilizer and water well so the entire root zone stays moist during the growing season. Sour gum is a native tree in many eastern wooded areas, and is nearly always found growing close to water.

LANDSCAPE USE

If you are lucky enough to have a natural woodland setting with a stream, you have a perfect location for sour gum. Though it favors moist sites, don't be afraid to plant it in a constantly wet low spot or even on a dry hillside if you have some irrigation. It will grow well in either location. The vivid fall color stands out among yellow-leafed trees such as ginkgo, golden larch, and European hornbeam as well as against the darker background of evergreen conifers. A wooded setting shelters sour gum from damaging winds. Rural or suburban areas are best since this tree languishes in the polluted air of cities.

Top Choices

- N. 'Jermyns Flame' has slightly larger leaves than the species. Fall foliage is stunning in shades of yellow, orange, and red.

- N. 'Sheffield Park' has the same rich fall color as the species but begins to show color about two weeks earlier.

FERTILIZING A TREE

Out of their native habitats, sour gum and other trees are deprived of the continuous supply of humus that accumulates on the forest floor. This organic duff, or leaf mold, holds moisture and releases nutrients. It also fertilizes and maintains healthy plants slowly yet steadily. The fertilizer spread on lawns is adequate for many trees, but sour gum seems to need its own dose every two or three years.

1 Drill holes about 12 inches deep, 1½ to 3 feet apart throughout the root zone.

2 Unless a soil test shows a specific deficiency, use a fertilizer with 1-2-1 ratio such as 5-10-5 (5 percent nitrogen, 10 percent phosphorus, 5 percent potassium). Apply in early spring to make nutrients available during the growing season. Use a slow-release organic product and follow application guidelines on the package to avoid burning the roots.

3 Cover holes with fertilizer in compost or with a similar organic soil amendment.

HOP HORNBEAM
Ostrya virginiana

Zones: 3–9

Type: Deciduous

Light: Full sun to part shade

Size: 25–40 ft. tall, 15–25 ft. wide

Form: Pyramidal to rounded

Growth Rate: Slow to moderate

Interest: Variable 2- to 4-in., dark green leaves, yellow in autumn; catkins in winter and spring; decorative hoplike fruit clusters in summer

The hop hornbeam combines a trouble-free disposition with good looks through four seasons. Its foliage is reminiscent of birch or elm, but its bark is rough, shaggy, and peeling. It lacks the disease problems that plague birch and elm and so is one of the best substitutes for either. The name derives from its dangling fruits, similar to the common hop, and from its *Carpinus caroliniana* relative, the hornbeam. Both are called ironwood because of their exceptionally hard wood.

HOW TO GROW

Once well established, hop hornbeam needs little more than routine care. It will grow in full or part sun, in any soil, but it prefers well-drained, slightly acidic soil in part shade. Add a layer of mulch to keep roots cool and water during long dry periods. If you are training a multistemmed seedling to tree form, make the cuts in winter. It is best to plant a young tree from a nursery can, allow it to grow for a year or two, then train it into one or several trunks.

LANDSCAPE USE

Hop hornbeam is a good choice for a multipurpose garden with a mix of small trees, shrubs, perennials, and bulbs. Sometimes an understory tree in its native habitats, hop hornbeam grows well in all but heavy shade. Strong branches make it a useful choice in high-wind areas. In a small plot, set shade-loving plants or blooming ornamentals off to the side; shade is too dense directly underneath for flowering plants. Keep hop hornbeam away from planting strips along streets where salt is applied in winter.

Shady Companions

Numerous garden-worthy woodland natives are easy-care filler plants for a shaded garden of trees. Consider perennials such as Solomon's-seal, shooting star, and rue anemone. Ferns are important for their long-lasting foliage and valuable texture. Ground covers help keep the soil surface cool, critical for roots of woodland trees. Taller shrubs, such as native azaleas and rhododendrons, add contours and fill in that middle space often left empty under high-branching trees.

A GARDEN OF TREES

A small tree like the hop hornbeam is the perfect addition to an informal setting as a structural element in a garden. Use it to line the borders of a property for a sense of enclosure or a garden room. Such a use defines space and creates an inner sanctuary at the same time. The low canopy muffles maximum sound from neighboring streets and roads. For a layered look and to show off foliage shrubs underneath, prune up the lower limbs.

Graceful and attractive, hop hornbeam provides a backdrop or starting point for a garden with trees. Add more elegant performers for contrast, such as a Japanese snowbell (*Styrax*) and several dogwoods (*Cornus*). Try to work in stalwart seasonal stars, such as the serviceberry tree and the almost treelike enkianthus and pieris shrubs as well.

SOURWOOD
Oxydendrum arboreum

Zones: 4–9

Type: Deciduous

Light: Full sun

Size: 25–40 ft. tall, 15–20 ft. wide

Form: Pyramidal to rounded

Growth Rate: Slow to moderate

Interest: Long, narrow leaves with good fall color; dangling flowers in summer; small brown fruits in winter

Sourwood's long, lustrous foliage is bright green in summer. It turns to brilliant yellow, scarlet, wine-red, and purple in early fall and is equally vibrant in the North and South. In midsummer, the canopy is nearly buried in a haze of tiny, urn-shaped flowers similar to heather and those of the strawberry tree. In autumn, small cream-colored small fruits stand out in dramatic contrast to the deeper leaf color. By winter, the hardened fruits turn brown and persist for a while on bare branches.

HOW TO GROW
Sourwood must have acidic soil with a pH below 6.5 (7.0 is neutral and above is alkaline). This eastern and southeastern native does best in the same conditions where rhododendrons and azaleas thrive: in moisture-retentive

soil that is well drained and fertile and contains ample peat or other organic matter. It will not thrive in heavy clay or dry soil.

Transplant only very young sourwood trees, before deep roots develop. Older trees cannot be easily moved and may not recover from the shock of being disturbed. After planting, keep the soil evenly moist and covered with an organic mulch such as chipped bark.

LANDSCAPE USE

Gardens large and small enjoy this modest-sized tree, which is never out of season. Size varies under cultivation, but it is usually under 25 feet until it is over fifty years old. Try to place it where there will be no activity under the canopy so that you can leave the lower branches intact. They give the tree a charming character and, more important, help to develop a stronger trunk. The lacy effect during blossom time is greatest when the foliage is low and nearly skirting the ground. Sourwood is particularly lovely in a prominent location at the edge of a lawn, either as a single specimen or in a group. It does best in full sun; flowering and color diminish in shade.

A Honey of a Tree

It may be surprising that ornamental trees are honey producers, but many species attract bees with their flowers. Sour gum (*Nyssa*) and linden (*Tilia*) are two that are rich in nectar. Sourwood—sour for the taste of the leaves—seems to be misnamed when you taste its delicious honey, which is produced commercially in the southern Appalachians.

A STAR FOR THE SPOTLIGHT

One of the best ornamental trees, sourwood deserves all the attention you can give it. A sure way to highlight its beauty is to uplight it with multiple fixtures. Uplighting is a type of indirect illumination that creates a mood in the evening garden unattainable in the bright sun. The light doesn't glare and the source isn't visible. The effect is practical as well as aesthetic.

By screening spotlights with low shrubs, benches, or other hardscape at ground level, you can dramatically accent sourwood's features each season. Locate fixtures at the base of the tree to highlight the tree's structure, and at a distance to emphasize the foliage, flowers, and fruits.

PERSIAN PARROTIA

Parrotia persica

Zones: 4–8

Type: Deciduous

Light: Full sun to light shade

Size: 20–40 ft. tall, 15–30 ft. wide

Form: Upright and oval or horizontal and spreading

Growth Rate: Slow

Interest: Deep green leaves that develop brilliant fall tints; beautiful bark; small red spring flowers

Persian parrotia is one of the best small trees for four-season interest. In late winter or very early spring, red tufts appear along with fuzzy brown bracts. Purplish red leaves unfold on the slightly pendulous branches, then turn glossy green in summer. The rich amber and gold, deep rose, orange, and scarlet autumn colors are superb. Distinctive bark, most visible in winter, shows mottled patterns as the outer green layer flakes off to expose a lighter grayish white skin beneath.

HOW TO GROW

Success with Persian parrotia depends on three basic conditions: slightly acidic soil, excellent drainage, and ample moisture after planting. A certain amount of alkalinity can be tolerated, but it may lessen the intensity of fall color. There is no leeway on the drainage or moisture for a young tree—plants in saturated conditions will succumb to rot; a mature specimen is more able to adapt to dry conditions. The root zone will stay moist longer with a 2- to 4-inch layer of mulch spread over the soil surface.

LANDSCAPE USE

There are two distinctly different forms of parrotia, each with its own beauty and its own place in the landscape. One is basically vertical, maturing into an oval outline; the other spreads widely, with multiple stems and tiers of horizontal branches. To grow as a single-trunked tree, a shrubby parrotia must be pruned to shape, either by you or in the nursery. It is most attractive in an open lawn or in a large bed unencumbered by other trees. Use it with low-growing shrubs and perennials. Give a specimen tree a clear site so its long branches will not interfere with buildings or other plants.

Top Choice

- *P.* 'Pendula', a weeping form, is more compact and easy to place in small gardens. It is worth tracking down if you don't have room for the species.

PATTERNS AND SILHOUETTES

Persian parrotia is strikingly beautiful when illuminated in the evening garden. In all seasons, even in winter, this tree can be an outdoor centerpiece with a focus on its irregular branching patterns and distinguishing decorative bark.

Create a dramatic mood in the night garden by hiding the light source. Conceal an upward-facing spotlight near the base of the trunk to highlight the intricate green, gray, and pinkish tan patchwork patterns of parrotia bark. For a silhouette effect, keep most of the light in the background.

Install your own lighting plan or have one customized, using a low-voltage 12-volt system or a line-voltage 120-volt system.

To conceal the fixtures, try one of the following options:

- Place fixtures behind painted metal or wooden shields in colors that blend with greenery or woody stems.

- Hide lights in a chimney tile.

- Make an artificial boulder out of a hypertufa mixture (cement, sand, and peat moss) for a light-weight piece of hardscape. Leave an opening in the back and hide the light inside.

SPRUCE

Picea

Zones: 3–7

Type: Evergreen

Light: Full sun

Size: 30–100 ft. tall, 15–30 ft. wide

Form: Pyramidal or conical

Growth Rate: Slow to moderate

Interest: Short, stiff, sometimes prickly needles; decorative cones

Shapely, uniform spruces have the convenient habit of retaining their basic appearance as they mature. Only the height and width change; the shape stays the same. Branches can be stiff and horizontal or gracefully ascending, often with drooping twiglets. Needles fill the twigs in bristling spirals, leaving tiny bumps, or pegs, after they fall. Papery, drooping cones near the ends of branches add decorative interest and attract birds and squirrels in winter.

HOW TO GROW

Spruce trees grow best in full sun in well-drained, acidic soil. Their roots are shallow and spreading and prefer a sandy loam soil, though they tolerate ordinary soils if amended with some organic matter. Spruces transplant well. Container-grown trees should be under 3 feet tall when planted to be sure the roots have not become restricted in the pot. Larger trees should be purchased balled-and-burlapped. Keep plants well watered, especially in dry times. Spruces grow best in cool northern areas.

LANDSCAPE USE

The dense foliage and thick branching of spruces makes these attractive trees a good choice for tall hedges and screens. They are especially suited for privacy screens along property lines or windbreaks on breezy ridges. Spruces are large trees that need space to grow and are not suited for small properties.

Top Choices

- *P. omorika,* Serbian spruce, thrives in a wider range of soils and conditions, including urban environments, than most spruces. Its short, upturned branches and beautiful dark green needles make it one of the most graceful conifers. Zones 4 to 8.

- *P. orientalis,* Oriental spruce, is a slow-growing species with very short and dense lustrous needles that give the tree a neat, compact appearance. Decorative cones grow 2 to 4 inches long at branch tips, turning from reddish purple to reddish brown. Zones 5 to 7.

GETTING THE BLUES

- Colorado spruce, *P. pungens,* is popular for its symmetrical, wedding-cake layers of blue foliage. The plants are native to the Rocky Mountains of North America. Seed-grown trees often have bluish new growth that fades to green with age. Many newer varieties have more intense coloration that provides interest throughout the year. Zones 2 to 7.

- *P.* 'Bizon Blue' reaches 35 to 40 feet tall with a uniform, pyramidal habit and bold, steel blue foliage.

- *P.* 'Hoopsii' has vivid whitish blue foliage and a dense, pyramidal form. It has been a popular variety for many years and is one of the best for color.

- *P.* 'Moerheimii' grows to about 30 feet tall with bright blue-gray foliage that retains good color through winter.

- *P.* 'Thompsonii' is a nicely symmetrical tree with thick needles of an intense whitish blue. It is one of the best varieties to choose for blue color.

DWARF CONIFERS
Picea spp. and others

Zones: 3–9

Type: Evergreen

Light: Full sun

Size: 2–10 ft. tall, 5–10 ft. wide

Form: Compact, spreading

Growth Rate: Slow

Interest: Rock gardens, shrub borders, specimen, wildlife gardens

Dwarf conifers, with their colorful needled foliage, add interest to gardens and landscapes every season of the year. These versatile but diminutive plants are available in a wide array of shapes and sizes to complement nearly every yard or garden. The plants derive from a number of different trees, from spruces and pines to firs and hemlocks, but have one thing in common: They are all small. They grow slowly enough to provide years of enjoyment without becoming overgrown and unsightly.

HOW TO GROW
Dwarf conifers generally can be purchased as container-grown plants and sometimes balled-and-burlapped for the larger forms. All types prefer full sun but many also do well in part shade. Plant dwarf conifers in well-drained,

acidic soil that has been amended with some organic matter such as rotted manure. Add a layer of acidic mulch, such as pine needles or shredded pine bark, after planting and renew each spring and fall. Keep plants well watered for the first two to three years and during dry periods. Fertilize lightly with an acidic fertilizer in spring as new growth begins. As a general rule, avoid planting dwarf conifers near roadways where salt is used in winter, or along walkways where shoveled snow could be piled on them.

Landscape Use

Dwarf conifers seem to be made for rock gardens, where their evergreen foliage highlights flowering plants and provides winter interest. They add contrast to shrub and perennial borders and make interesting small specimen plants.

Top Choices

- *Picea abies* 'Nidiformis', bird's nest spruce, forms a flat-topped mound with dark green foliage that eventually reaches 2 to 3 feet tall. Zones 2 to 7.

- *Picea glauca* var. *albertiana* 'Conica', dwarf Alberta spruce, has soft green needles and a formal, pyramidal shape reaching 8 to 10 feet tall. Zones 2 to 6.

MORE DWARF CONIFERS

- *Chamaecyparis obtusa* 'Nana Gracilis' is a dwarf Hinoki false cypress that grows 4 feet tall with flat sprays of dark green foliage. Zones 4 to 8.

- *Chamaecyparis pisifera* 'Plumosa Compressa Aurea' is a tiny thing, just 8 inches tall, with yellow-green foliage. Zones 4 to 8.

- *Juniperus squamata* 'Blue Star' grows slowly (1 to 2 feet) with silver-blue foliage. Zones 4 to 7.

- *Pinus densiflora* 'Soft Green', a dwarf form of Japanese red pine with bright green foliage, reaches up to 6 feet tall. Zones 3 to 7.

- *Pinus strobus* 'Pygmaea' is a very dwarf, mounded form of white pine with dark green foliage. Zones 3 to 8.

- *Thuja occidentalis* 'Rheingold', Rheingold arborvitae, reaches 4 feet tall with sprays of rich golden foliage. Zones 3 to 8.

- *Thuja orientalis* 'Aurea Nana' grows to about 3 feet tall with attractive vertical fans of soft golden foliage. Zones 6 to 9.

- *Tsuga canadensis* 'Jeddeloh' has light green foliage and a mounding habit. It grows 1 to 2 feet tall. Zones 4 to 7.

PINE
Pinus

Zones: 3–8

Type: Evergreen

Light: Full sun

Size: 20–100 ft. tall, 20–40 ft. wide

Form: Pyramidal to irregular and rounded

Growth Rate: Slow to fast

Interest: Green needles with 2, 3, or 5 in a bundle; interesting bark patterns; decorative cones

Mention the words *evergreen conifer* and pine is often what springs to mind. Many pines have intriguing shapes, unique textures, or fast growth that makes them ideal specimen trees. Though many grow naturally to over 100 feet tall, their size under cultivation is routinely lower. Some of the best pines remain under 50 feet tall. Regardless of their eventual height, pines add a graceful presence to the landscape.

HOW TO GROW

Just as there are considerable visual differences among pine species, there are variations in cultural requirements as well. Generally, pines grow well in rich or poor soil. Most require good drainage, but some such as white pine can also thrive in wetlands. Rank growth results from overfertilization, drought, and poor air quality more than lack of fertility. Stressed trees are susceptible to insect and disease problems, such as beetles and rust. In cooler regions do not plant near roadways, because salt can brown the needles.

LANDSCAPE USE

Pines make excellent specimen trees for large properties. Kept trimmed, they are suitable for hedges and screens. Group plantings provide food and cover for birds and other wildlife.

Top Choices

- *P. bungeana*, lacebark pine, is a three-needle, dark green pine that begins branching close to the ground. It is a pyramidal shape in youth, then broadens to become an open, airy, flat-topped tree about 40 feet tall. Lacebark pine has greenish white bark that flakes off in lacy patterns. Zones 4 to 8.

- *P. densiflora*, Japanese red pine, has attractive reddish bark and an irregular shape. It commonly develops several trunks at ground level and grows rapidly into an irregular and broad-topped 50-foot-tall tree. It does not do well in arid regions or in strong winds. Zones 4 to 7. The variety 'Umbraculifera', Tanyosho pine, has an umbrella shape and grows 25 feet tall. It is excellent for use in Japanese gardens. Zones 5 to 7.

- *P. cembra*, Swiss stone pine, is a picturesque, slow-growing tree to 35 feet tall with dense, dark green foliage and an upright habit. Zones 4 to 7.

A PLETHORA OF PINES

- *P. leucodermis*, Bosnian pine, grows slowly to 40 feet with dark, glossy foliage and young cones colored purple-blue. Zones 4 to 6.

- *P. strobus*, Eastern white pine, has a graceful, pyramidal shape with soft green needles. It is a large tree reaching 50 to 80 feet tall. Eastern white pine grows best in the East and upper Midwest. 'Brevifolia Elf' is smaller than the species but with a similar form that reaches 20 feet tall. 'Fastigiata' has a columnar shape growing to 45 feet tall and makes a good screen. Zones 3 to 8.

- *P. thunbergiana*, Japanese black pine, has an open, roughly pyramidal shape and grows 20 to 80 feet tall. It is very tolerant of salt spray, wind, and sandy soils, making it an excellent choice for coastal gardens. 'Angelica's Thunderhead' is a strange name for an attractive tree; the new growth, or candles, are pure white, maturing to deep green. 'Majestic Beauty' has dark green foliage and tolerates air pollution. Zones 6 to 8.

WEEPING CONIFERS
Pinus spp. and others

Zones: 3–8

Type: Evergreen

Light: Full to part sun

Size: 10–20 ft. tall

Form: Weeping

Growth Rate: Slow to fast

Interest: Graceful habit; dark, glossy evergreen foliage

If you want your yard or garden to have a feeling of gracefulness and motion, plant a weeping conifer. These plants derive from many different species, from hemlocks to pines. What they have in common is their unique growth habit. Weeping conifers are often used as the centerpiece of a landscape design. Their flowing shape and drooping evergreen branches provide visual interest and texture every season of the year.

HOW TO GROW
Weeping conifers prefer well-drained, acidic soil that is rich in organic matter. Cover the root area with an acidic mulch such as pine needles or shredded pine bark at planting time and renew each spring. Plants in full sun are often more vigorous and resist pests and disease

somewhat better than those in part shade. Fertilizer is usually not required. Some varieties can be trained on a trellis or against a wall, making an attractive and unusual background for flower gardens. Others need their trunks staked when young to develop a strong central stem that can support the heavy canopy of foliage. Left untrained, these varieties can be used as interesting ground covers.

LANDSCAPE USE
Weeping conifers make excellent specimen plants in a lawn or a small island bed. They are good focal points for Japanese, rock, or water gardens. When used in the shrub border, weeping conifers provide a dark green background for flowering shrubs while softening the lines of more upright plants.

Top Choices

- *Abies concolor* 'Gables Weeping', weeping white fir, is a slow-growing tree with drooping branches of blue-green foliage. Zones 3 to 7.

- *Picea abies* 'Inversa' and 'Pendula' are weeping Norway spruces. They are characterized by a slender, weeping trunk and drooping branches. To showcase their form, train or stake them. Left untrained, they make a nice ground cover. Zones 2 to 6.

- *Picea glauca* 'Pendula', weeping white spruce, is a variety with a narrow shape and drooping branches covered with grayish green needles. Zones 3 to 6.

MORE WEEPING CONIFERS

- *Picea pungens* 'Glauca Pendula', weeping blue spruce, has a graceful, slender trunk and prickly, blue-gray needles on very pendulous branches. The trunk can be trained or staked to produce a weeping form, or left unsupported and grown as a ground cover. Zones 2 to 7.

- *Picea pungens* 'Shilo-Weeping', Shilo weeping blue spruce, has a strong, upright trunk and weeping branches. Zones 2 to 7.

- *Pinus densiflora* 'Pendula', weeping Japanese red pine, can be staked into a weeping tree. Left untrained, it makes a nice ground cover. It has dark green needles and attractive reddish bark. Zones 5 to 7.

- *Pinus strobus* 'Pendula', weeping white pine, has an undulating, graceful trunk with many long, drooping branches that touch the ground. The tree needs to be trained when young to produce the best form. Zones 3 to 8.

- *Tsuga canadensis* 'Sargentii' is a beautiful tree that forms a dense, spreading mound of weeping branches up to 10 feet tall and 20 feet wide. Small needles hold their dark green color all year. Zones 3 to 7.

CHINESE PISTACHE
Pistacia chinensis

Zones: 6–9

Type: Deciduous

Light: Full sun

Size: 30–60 ft. tall, 30–35 ft. wide

Form: Irregular in youth, round with age

Growth Rate: Moderate

Interest: Compound leaves, brightly colored in fall; insignificant flowers; large clusters of nutlike fruits

This is a nearly perfect tree for the West and South. It endures drought with no ill effects (save slow growth) and needs little care after planting. In addition, Chinese pistache is pest-free, wind tolerant, and thrives in urban conditions. Fall color—a beautiful burst of orange-red—is an added bonus. In the presence of male trees, females produce bright red berries that ripen to purple. Young trees tend to look awkward and unbalanced, but after a few years the canopy fills out to a rounded crown.

HOW TO GROW

Tolerant and adaptable, Chinese pistache will grow in soil that is fertile or poor, acidic or alkaline, moist or dry—as long as it is well drained. It prefers warm climates to cooler coastal areas, thriving even where summer heat is intense. Drought tolerance is greatest where loose soils allow deep root penetration.

Many young trees need staking and pruning to help them achieve an attractive shape. (See "Staking a Tree," page 31.) Some pruning may be needed to train a single leader, remove excess branching on main limbs, and shorten side branches. Prune during the dormant season when you can easily see the branching structure.

LANDSCAPE USE

Chinese pistache grows well in a lawn, as a street tree, in open sites, or in filtered shade. It is good for dry spots, supplying a lush look despite its low water requirements. The neat canopy looks good in a row planting along a roadway, street, or fence line. In a drought-tolerant garden, you can also plant native ceanothus and snowberry (*Symphoricarpos albus*), manzanita (*Arctostaphylos*), juniper, wild buckwheat (*Eriogonum*), and ornamental grass. All of these plants have species and varieties that require no irrigation after they become established.

Top Choice

- *P. vera,* pistachio, is smaller and not as ornamental as its Chinese cousin but is valued for its edible nuts. To get a nut crop, you must plant a male tree as well as a female. 'Peters' is the most common male variety; 'Kerman' is a widely grown female (nut-producing) variety. Zones 9 to 10.

CHOOSING A STREET TREE

Trees planted along a city street play many of the same roles as lawn trees. They add important height, provide shady relief from reflected sun, and improve the ambience of the environment.

Many trees are eminently suitable for street planting; Chinese pistache is one of them as long as no overhead utility wires will be threatened by its eventual height. It is practical along streets in urban areas for its:

- easy tolerance of urban smog and poor soil, including alkalinity, a common problem near concrete;

- brilliant fall color, widely and enthusiastically admired;

- deep rooting below sidewalks or paving;

- low maintenance and drought tolerance;

- mature, high, vertical branching for gentle, filtered shade plus free movement of any size of vehicle underneath;

- handsome fissured bark and reddish twigs when out of leaf in winter.

FLOWERING CHERRY
Prunus

Zones: 4–9

Type: Deciduous

Light: Full sun

Size: 20–50 ft. tall, 20–40 ft. wide

Form: Upright to spreading and rounded

Growth Rate: Fast

Interest: Glossy green leaves, fall color; white or pink spring flowers; decorative bark

In midspring, flowering cherries stand out as frothy, hazy clouds of blossoms. Flowering cherries don't stop with a one-season show. Most species have attractive foliage with yellowish orange-to-red tints in fall. The bark of many flowering cherries is smooth and glossy, like polished mahogany, while others have thin, peeling bark. The attractive branches and trunks add color to the landscape all winter long.

HOW TO GROW

Plant flowering cherry trees in well-drained soil that neither dries out completely nor becomes waterlogged. Stressed trees can be susceptible to insect and disease problems, making the trees short lived. Healthy trees can live for decades. Prune to shape immediately after flowering.

Remove dead or damaged branches anytime. Trees do best in neutral soil, lightly fertilized; their roots can take competition from nearby plants.

LANDSCAPE USE

Flowering cherries are stunning specimen plants and are most often used alone in a lawn or as the anchor of a small island bed. You can also use their exuberant flowering as a centerpiece in a spring bed or border. For added color, underplant with spring bulbs such as tulips.

Top Choices

- *P. sargentii,* sargent cherry, is fast growing and reaches 40 to 50 feet tall. In midspring, clusters of single, deep pink blossoms cover the tree in a lavish floral display. The foliage emerges purplish green in spring and turns flame red in autumn. Sargent cherry has beautiful lenticel-studded, mahogany-red bark and is an excellent flowering cherry for the North. 'Columnaris' has a narrow, upright shape, and 'Rancho' has a vase-shaped form. Zones 4 to 7.

- *P. x yedoensis,* Yoshino cherry, is one of the best known of the flowering cherries from its high profile along the Tidal Basin in Washington, D.C. The variety 'Snow Fountains' (also called 'White Fountain') is a weeping form reaching 6 to 12 feet tall. Its cascading branches are covered with single, white flowers in spring. It tolerates heat, humidity, and drought. Zones 5 to 8.

DOUBLE-FLOWERING CHERRIES

- Higan cherry (*P. subhirtella*) 'Rosy Cloud' is a lovely tree with large, double, deep pink flowers over a long period. 'Autumnalis' is another variety with pale pink, semidouble flowers; it blooms sparsely in fall as well as fully in spring. Both tolerate heat and cold—but not smog or wind—better than most flowering cherries. Zones 4 to 9.

- Sato Zakura Flowering Cherries (formerly *P. serrulata*) are usually grafted onto a *Prunus* rootstock about 6 feet above the ground where they begin branching, giving them a unique appearance among flowering trees.

- The variety 'Kwanzen' (also called 'Sekiyama') is the hardiest, most popular of a group called 'Kwanzen'. One of the most vigorous reaches 30 to 40 feet tall. Clusters of 2-inch, double, pink blossoms cover the branches of 'Kwanzen' in spring. The plants have bronze-red fall foliage and tolerate heat and humidity. Zones 5 to 8.

PURPLE-LEAF PLUM

Prunus

Zones: 5–8

Type: Deciduous

Light: Full sun

Size: 7–25 ft. tall, 6–20 ft. wide

Form: Upright to spreading and rounded

Growth Rate: Moderate to fast

Interest: Glossy purple leaves; white or pink spring flowers; small fruits in late summer

Purple-leaf plums are the mainstay of many landscapes. The dark burgundy to purple foliage stays vibrant and colorful from spring to fall. Purple-leaf plums are small trees, most growing to between 15 and 25 feet tall with some just 7 to 10 feet tall. In early spring the branches are decorated with small, starry white or pink flowers. In late summer small, 1-inch plums appear that persist on the tree for many weeks.

HOW TO GROW

Purple-leaf plums have the brightest-colored foliage when grown in full sun. They lose some of their ornamental value and color when grown in part shade. Plant in well-drained soil that is not too rich. The trees do well during hot summers if they receive regular watering.

Prune wayward branches or lightly shape trees after flowering is complete in spring. Purple-leaf plums are more susceptible to insect and disease problems if the trees are under stress. Regular watering, light spring fertilizing, and lots of sunshine keep the plants healthy, vigorous, and less subject to problems.

LANDSCAPE USE

Widely used as foundation plants, purple-leaf plums soften the corners of buildings or provide color to the facades of homes and outbuildings. Planted in groups in lawns, the trees are vivid islands of glossy purple in a sea of green. Purple-leaf plums are nice additions to the shrub border, with dwarf forms a fine background for perennial beds.

Top Choices

- P. x *cerasifera* 'Atropurpurea' has an upright habit with new leaves colored wine-red, darkening to purple with age. Fruits are purple.

- P. x c. 'Mt. Saint Helens' is a very vigorous, strong tree with pale pink early-spring flowers and rich purple foliage.

- P. x c. 'Thundercloud' bears pink blossoms in early spring before leaves emerge. Foliage is a deep, glossy purple.

SMALLER PLUMS

For a bold dash of purple in a small yard, nothing does it better than a dwarf purple-leafed plum.

- P. x *cistena*, dwarf purple-leaf plum, is a cold-loving small tree reaching 8 to 15 feet tall. The flowers are white to pale pink, opening in early spring before the leaves emerge. Foliage is a deep wine-purple from spring to fall. Zones 3 to 8.

- P. x *cerasifera* 'Newport' grows to 15 feet tall with pale blush to white flowers and bronze-purple foliage. Zones 4 to 8.

- P. x c. 'Purple Pony' is a genetic dwarf that matures to only 10 or 12 feet tall. It holds its deep purple leaf color through the season. Flowers are pale pink.

- P. x *blireiana*, Blireiana plum, has purple leaves that gradually turn green in summer. The light pink, double flowers appear in early spring before the leaves. Fruits are reddish but are usually hidden by the thick foliage. Zones 5 to 8.

- P. 'Moseri' bears small, light pink, double flowers on strong, vigorous branches. Foliage stays purple for a longer time than Blireiana plum. Zones 5 to 8.

GOLDEN LARCH
Pseudolarix kaempferi

Zones: 4–8

Type: Deciduous

Light: Full sun

Size: 30–50 ft. tall, 20–40 ft. wide

Form: Broadly pyramidal

Growth Rate: Slow

Interest: Short, light green needles, golden yellow in fall; yellow catkins; flower-like cones

The name *Pseudolarix kaempferi* means "false larch." This tree is easier to use in landscapes than the true larches (*Larix*) because it grows more slowly, staying below 50 feet even after a hundred years. It is also more open branched and less weeping and has narrower individual needles. Foliage is a fresh light green above, blue-green below; in fall it turns vibrant golden yellow with hints of orange. The long, soft needles drop after a few weeks of autumn color.

HOW TO GROW

Golden larch adapts to every type of soil except those high in lime. Deep, well-drained soil, rich with organic matter and evenly moistened, is best. Fertilize every few years if foliage is thin and growth is not noticeable. Give this tree some shelter from cold, drying winds, but keep it in an open spot in full sun. It is quite tolerant of summer heat.

Allow only one central leader to develop. If a second one appears, cut it out to prevent a weak crotch from forming. A broad-based pyramid is the natural shape. Remove or shorten the lowest branches if they spread too widely, but do no other pruning.

LANDSCAPE USE

The soft green spring and summer foliage and its glittering golden yellow color in fall are enough to elevate this tree to a special status. The shapely, balanced outline, however, is also rewarding in the landscape and striking in a lawn. If you have the space, plant a group of three golden larches 20 to 25 feet apart. The horizontal branches, somewhat pendulous at the tips, make an attractive pattern against a turf background or, even better, against darker conifers such as yew, cedar, or cypress. There are also dwarf cultivars available.

Top Choices

- *Larix kaempferi,* Japanese larch, grows quickly to 80 feet but is otherwise similar to golden larch. Give it a site with moist, acidic soil to prevent pest problems. Zones 4 to 7.

- *L. decidua,* European larch, grows almost as tall and is good for cold climates (as long as it has moist to wet, acidic soil). 'Pendula' is a weeping form. Zones 2 to 6.

COLORFUL CONIFERS

Not all conifers are evergreen—golden larch drops its leaves each fall and sends out new needles in spring. And not all conifers are green—golden larch turns bright golden yellow in autumn. Using this tree and other colorful conifers to advantage in your garden provides a wealth of interest year-round.

Conifer foliage can be just as ornamental as a flowering tree or a bright, broadleafed canopy. Unlike golden larch, most conifers hold their distinctive hues all year.

Certain species, such as cedars and pines, vary mostly from light and dark green to shades of blue, whereas many *Chamaecyparis* and yew cultivars offer reddish purple, yellow, bright gold, and green-black shades as well.

Golden larch supplies a burst of fall color that can rival that of any broadleafed tree— plus it turns late in the season, often igniting as other trees lose their leaves.

WHITE OAK

Quercus spp.

Zones: 3–9

Type: Deciduous

Light: Full sun

Size: 50–80 ft. tall, 50–80 ft. wide

Form: Pyramidal to spreading and rounded

Growth Rate: Slow to moderate

Interest: Glossy green, usually lobed leaves, erratic fall color; sturdy branching; acorns in fall

Oaks are a large group of trees with species that grow from 6 feet to over 100 feet tall. Some of the most ornamental belong to a group called the white oaks, named for the light, whitish gray color of the bark. The leaves of white oaks have rounded lobes and turn reddish purple in fall. These magnificent trees grow in diverse climates and conditions and are valued everywhere for their shade.

HOW TO GROW

Choose a white oak that will thrive in your climate and planting site. If problems with gypsy moth or oak wilt disease are prevalent in your area, opt for a species that is resistant. Try to plant a young tree or, if time is not a factor, grow from an acorn to avoid disturbing the deep roots. Though some, such as California white oaks, tolerate some drought, the trees featured here thrive in deep, fertile, moist, and acidic soil; they become seriously chlorotic in alkaline soils. Give them full sun in a site that will stay undisturbed for the life of the tree. Disturbing soil in the root zone severely damages roots and shortens their life.

LANDSCAPE USE

White oaks make excellent shade trees and are well suited for large yards and properties. Oaks attract songbirds in spring (they feed on inchworms) and squirrels in fall as the acorns ripen.

Top Choices

- *Q. alba,* white oak, is grand and stately, assuming giant proportions in eastern and midwestern woodlands but unlikely to exceed 50 to 80 feet in home landscapes. With unfettered space to spread roots and limbs, it can live to great age. Fall color at its best is orange-red to purple, but more often is reddish brown.

- *Q. bicolor,* swamp white oak, can take both swampy conditions and some drought as well as poor and compacted soil, which makes it suitable for urban sites. It is easier to transplant and develops superior fall color, but the overall shape is not quite as refined as *Q. alba.* Zones 3 to 8.

OTHER OAKS

- Upright English oak, *Q. robur* 'Fastigiata', is a form of the ancient English oak that looks more like a European hornbeam with its smooth oval outline and narrow, tall habit. Grafted trees are rigidly upright, whereas seed-grown specimens are more irregular. Well suited for formal gardens in long rows and corner plantings, this tree can also be used in narrow spaces and in groups as a vertical screen. Be sure to give it good air circulation to cut down on the incidence of powdery mildew. Zones 4 to 8.

- Bur oak, *Q. macrocarpa*, is a large shade tree reaching 75 feet tall. Also called mossy-cup oak, it is very long lived with specimens over three hundred years old. The leaves are rounded with irregular scallops along the margins. They turn yellowish brown in fall. Plant bur oak when young, because it is difficult to transplant when older. It thrives in slightly acidic to slightly alkaline soils, and even grows well in heavy clay soils. Bur oak is a popular shade tree in the Midwest. Zones 3 to 8.

RED OAK
Quercus spp.

Zones: 4–9

Type: Deciduous

Light: Full sun

Size: 50–80 ft. tall, 50–80 ft. wide

Form: Pyramidal to spreading and rounded

Growth Rate: Moderate to fast

Interest: Glossy green, usually lobed leaves, erratic fall color; sturdy branching; acorns in fall

Symbols of natural beauty, strength, and endurance, red oaks are fast-growing, stately trees with multiple uses, from shading a country yard to lining a city street. Red oaks have leaves with pointed lobes tipped with a slender hair. Though their noble size and shade-giving disposition take time to develop, red oaks always hold a promise for the future, unfolding great beauty as they mature into handsome trees.

HOW TO GROW
Red oaks do not have the pronounced taproot of white oaks and are often easier to transplant. They need full sun and well-drained, acidic soil. In neutral or alkaline soils the leaves will turn yellow. Depending on the species, red oaks thrive in a range of soils, from sandy

loam for red and scarlet oaks to heavy wet clay for pin oak. Most tolerate some urban pollution.

LANDSCAPE USE

Red oaks are tall, broad, long-lived shade trees that are excellent for the large yard. Because they tolerate some pollution, they also make good street trees. Some red oaks, such as scarlet oak, do well in sandy soil and are good choices for coastal properties.

Top Choices

- *Q. palustris*, pin oak, is always distinctively pyramidal in youth. This fast-growing tree eventually becomes rounded in maturity. Wide spreading at the base of its crown (25 to 40 feet), the slender horizontal limbs droop slightly while the uppermost branches are short and vertical. Fall color tends to be rich red, though copper and bronze tones are not uncommon. Pin oaks have narrow, deeply cut leaves that usually persist through winter. Zones 4 to 9.

- *Q. rubra*, red oak, grows quickly into a rounded tree. Its shiny, pointed, and lobed leaves are known for their reddish tint in spring and bright red to russet-brown fall color. This is a superb shade tree in a spacious lawn where there is room for its broad crown. Width usually equals height, about 75 feet. It will tolerate limited drought after it is well established. Zones 4 to 8.

RED OAKS FOR WARM CLIMATES

- Southern red oak, Q. *falcata,* has wide, deeply lobed leaves. Also called Spanish oak, it thrives in poor, dry, or sandy soils, making it a good choice for conservation plantings in warm regions. The tree eventually reaches 70 feet tall with a spreading, rounded crown. Zones 7 to 9.

- Scarlet oak, Q. *coccinea,* can be planted as an alternative to the pin oak for its greater tolerance of dry and alkaline soils and bright autumn color. The trees are easy to transplant. Scarlet oak is as good an addition to coastal gardens or grouped on slopes to prevent erosion. Zones 4 to 9.

- Chinese evergreen oak, Q. *myrsinifolia,* is one of the most graceful and hardiest of the evergreen oaks because it keeps its leaves year-round. The leaves are glossy dark green on a tree that grows to 30 feet tall. It is an excellent street tree for the South. Chinese evergreen oak is often labeled as blue Japanese oak or Japanese evergreen oak in nurseries, but these are different species. Zones 7 to 9.

Japanese Umbrella Pine
Sciadopitys verticillata

Zones: 5–9

Type: Evergreen

Light: Full sun to light shade

Size: 20–60 ft. tall, 15–20 ft. wide

Form: Compact and conical, then upright and spreading

Growth Rate: Slow

Interest: Glossy, flat green needles in whorls; cones green for a year, then brown

Japanese umbrella pine is one of the most distinctive landscape trees, both beautiful and curious. Actually, it is not a pine at all, but is more closely related to trees of ancient origin, the dawn redwood and sequoia—members of the bald cypress family. Foliage is scaly along the branches with longer, more pinelike needles bunched at ends in tufts radiating like umbrella spokes. Japanese umbrella pine takes twenty years to reach 10 feet and sometimes develops several trunks.

How to Grow
A newly planted umbrella pine must have constantly moist, well-drained soil for at least two years until it is fully established; water regularly thereafter to keep it looking its best. To sustain the greatest vigor, give it a

protected location with morning sun and afternoon shade in organically enriched, acidic soil. Renew a surface mulch over the root zone each spring. Hot, dry, windy sites cause stress and performance problems.

LANDSCAPE USE

Japanese umbrella pine bears some of the most attractive foliage among the evergreen coniferous trees and is one of the best accent plants for the garden. Its unusual texture is sure to attract attention. Since it grows so slowly, you can freely garden around it as a shrub for many years before it achieves much height. The limbs are filled out from the ground up, and growth is usually no more than 6 inches a year. Given the right conditions, Japanese umbrella pine is long lived. Older trees show more of their bark than young specimens, because their habit loosens and branches open up. On these trees, the brownish red, peeling bark adds to the character and appeal.

Top Choices

- *S.* 'Aurea' and 'Ossorio Gold' bear needles with yellow tones.

- *S.* 'Variegata' foliage is a mixture of solid greens and yellows and green-and-cream variegation.

- *S.* 'Wintergreen' holds its natural green color best in cold northern climates.

MAINTENANCE CHORES

Japanese umbrella pine holds its needles for three growing seasons before replacing them. Over the years, the densely whorled branches can harbor accumulations of dead needles inside the foliage. As the needles and duff from bark and cones deteriorate over time, the decaying matter can foster fungal growth and threaten trees with disease.

It's a good idea to check inside the tree around the trunk every few years and clean out tight interiors. Remove clumps of dead-needle buildup near the base of branches and spread them as mulch on the ground beyond the drip line.

GIVE IT A "BATH"

Like many other evergreen conifers, Japanese umbrella pine thrives in cool, moist sites. Even when it is growing in a humid climate, it benefits from periodic extra moisture when rains are infrequent. Hose it down during warm weather or direct a sprinkler head toward the foliage. Be sure that it has good drainage to handle the runoff and that water does not stand at the base of the trunk. The spray will clean off any dust and bring out the luster in the needles.

JAPANESE PAGODA TREE
Sophora japonica

Zones: 4–8

Type: Deciduous

Light: Full sun

Size: 50–75 ft. tall, 50–75 ft. wide

Form: Rounded to broadly spreading

Growth Rate: Moderate to fast

Interest: Dark green, compound leaves; creamy, 12-in. flower panicles in summer; bean like pods in fall

Once commonly planted near Buddhist temples in Japan, this tree is popular in Europe and America. In mid- to late summer, showy flowers resembling creamy wisteria decorate the mature canopy. Yellow autumn foliage yields to seedpods that look like strings of beads and last all winter. The limbs, smooth and gray on young wood, darker and rougher on mature trees, arch high to form an open, domed interior, making this one of the best choices for filtered shade in hot-summer climates.

HOW TO GROW
Known as a tough survivor, Japanese pagoda tree thrives under most conditions but loses some of its appeal in excessive heat, cold, drought, or pollution. Plant it in full sun in average to fertile, well-drained soil, sheltered

from strong winds. Plant balled-and-burlapped or container-grown trees while they are young, before a long taproot develops.

To avoid freeze damage to young trees, protect them with burlap cages or spray the foliage with an antidesiccant for a few years. Trim off winter damage after growth begins in spring. Prune in fall to encourage high branching on a tall central leader. Thin the lower branches if they seem heavy and hang too low for convenience.

LANDSCAPE USE

Despite a minor litter nuisance, Japanese pagoda tree is widely planted as a street and patio tree. It allows comfortable, dappled sunlight through its open canopy, and its deep roots pose no threat to concrete, bricks, tile, or pavers. After blossoms drop, your patio will have an enchanting snowy carpet. In a lawn, the blossom and pod litter is easily picked up by a mower; it melds into chipped bark mulch in your garden.

Top Choices

- S. 'Regent' is faster growing and blooms at a younger age than the species. It is more vertically branching, has a narrower crown, and can be planted where head space is crowded.

- S. 'Princeton Upright' is similar but more compact.

WARM-CLIMATE FRAGRANCE

In mild climates (Zones 8 to 10), the Texas mountain laurel or mescal bean (*S. secundiflora*) is an excellent, sweetly scented flowering tree. It blooms much earlier than the Japanese pagoda tree and its foliage is thicker and darker green. The early-spring blossoms are similarly wisteria-like, but the panicles are shorter and the color is a rich violet-blue.

This species reaches only 15 to 25 feet tall, an asset in small gardens. Native to Texas and New Mexico, this tree needs loose, alkaline soil with fast drainage and some moisture. The small size and fragrant blossoms make a lovely addition to a patio. The bright red poisonous seeds are a drawback; if small children or pets are about, remove the pods before the seeds develop.

NO BLOOMS?

Don't be surprised if your Japanese pagoda tree does not flower reliably every year. Individual trees vary in their flowering habits and also are affected by the weather. You may have a tree that blooms heavily only in alternate years.

Korean Mountain Ash
Sorbus alnifolia

Zones: 3–7

Type: Deciduous

Light: Full sun

Size: 40–50 ft. tall, 20–30 ft. wide

Form: Pyramidal and upright to oval and rounded

Growth Rate: Moderate

Interest: Oval, bright green leaves with good fall color; creamy white spring flowers; red berries in fall

Korean mountain ash thrives only in cold to moderate climates, making it a good choice for parts of the North and the Pacific Northwest. Lustrous green in spring and summer, mountain ash foliage is among the best and brightest in the autumn landscape. It turns luminous shades of yellow-orange and orange-red, and is filled with pinkish red berries. Pale blossoms nearly cover the tree in spring.

How to Grow

Korean mountain ash grows well in full sun in average, well-drained soil, tolerating some acidity and alkalinity as well as some wetness and aridity. However, it does not tolerate drought, standing water, compacted soil, or poor drainage. It does well on the edge of woodlands, preferably remote from urban smog.

Mountain ash is susceptible to fire blight disease. To lessen the threat of infection, withhold all fertilizers and cut back diseased wood to 6 inches below the damaged tissue. (See page 117.) Pest and disease risk is always present in the landscape, but healthy, unstressed trees are unlikely targets. Borers, which infest some *Sorbus* species, seem to bypass this one.

LANDSCAPE USE

This delightful tree is easy to love in the right location. The flat, white flower clusters against riveting green foliage provide the greatest eye appeal in midspring. It is an ideal shade or specimen tree for backyard lawns, and it's good near outdoor activity areas where you can watch its decor change with the seasons. The dangling fruits feed resident birds through fall and into winter. Since mountain ash does not tolerate pollution of any kind, including smog and salt, keep it away from streetside locations.

Top Choice

• S. 'Redbird' has a narrow, upright form. Leaves turn gold in fall, forming a nice contrast to the abundant red berries.

EUROPEAN MOUNTAIN ASH

The handsome foliage on this cool-climate cousin, S. aucuparia, is more similar to its namesake trees in the ash (Fraxinus) genus. The leaves are long, compound, and feathery, imparting filtered summer shade. The European mountain ash thrives in Zones 3 to 6, where summer heat is not severe. In these northern climates, this is a three-season tree, in full bloom in late spring, full foliaged throughout summer, and in full berry and full golden orange color in autumn. Usually orange-red, the fruits on various cultivars range from apricot ('Apricot Queen') to yellow ('Xanthocarpa' and 'Brilliant Yellow') and brilliant red ('Cardinal Royal' and 'Red Copper Glow').

KEEP IT HAPPY

It is best to plant mountain ash only in northern climate zones where it is well adapted. It can be temperamental and prone to insect and disease attacks in urban smog and in alkaline or compacted soils. Loose, acidic soil is best. Under stressful growing conditions, this is a short-lived tree. When happily situated, it stands out as a valuable and comely addition to the landscape, one of the most appealing ornamental trees.

STEWARTIA

Stewartia pseudocamellia

Zones: 5–8

Type: Deciduous

Light: Full to part sun

Size: 20–40 ft. tall, 20–25 ft. wide

Form: Pyramidal to broadly rounded, single or multi-stemmed

Growth Rate: Slow

Interest: Elliptical, dark green leaves with good fall color; camellia-like summer blossoms; peeling bark

Many gardeners consider this the best landscape tree for year-round interest. As stewartia leafs out in spring, the foliage has wine to purple tints; the thick, somewhat dimpled leaves mature to a rich green. Its single, white, shallow-cupped blossoms resemble camellias. Bloom begins in mid- to late summer and extends over many weeks. Fall color is vibrant—sometimes yellows and oranges, more often reds and purple. As trees mature and trunks and limbs enlarge, the colorful bark becomes a principal feature. Tawny red-brown combines with olive, gray, and creamy yellow in mottled patterns as the bark chips and peels away, sculpting a muscular outline and creating an unforgettable impression.

HOW TO GROW

Stewartia grows best in acidic soil rich in organic matter. Loose loam or peat makes for easy root penetration, fast drainage, and the proper pH. (See "Testing Your Soil" at right.) Keep soil moist and the surface covered with a 2- to 3-inch layer of acidic organic mulch such as pine needles or pine bark. Plant stewartia away from drying winds; in hot climates, place it under a high canopy of deciduous trees to protect it from scorching summer sun. Low moisture, searing heat, and wind cause sufficient stress to stop growth. Your tree will take a year or two to become established; young trees planted from containers generally do best.

LANDSCAPE USE

Stewartia is prized as a specimen. This winsome tree can serve as an anchor in your landscape, delighting the eye each month of the year. It associates well with ground cover shrubs such as sweet box (*Sarcococca* spp.) as well as taller species like rhododendron. Older trees are important for their shade as well as their visual impact.

Top Choice

- *S. Koreana*, Korean stewartia, is a little smaller than its Japanese relative but otherwise very similar. It does best in Zones 5 to 7.

TESTING YOUR SOIL

An acidic soil with a pH in the 4.5 to 6.0 range is critical for success with stewartia. Test your soil before planting and add acid-reacting amendments if necessary. You can apply sulfur at the rate of 10 to 20 pounds per 1,000 square feet to increase acidity. Be sure to mix amendments deeply into a large area while the soil is moist. To conduct a valid soil test:

1 Gather soil with a trowel or core sampler from several spots throughout the planting area, 6 to 12 inches below the surface.

2 Mix these samples together in a clean bucket, then remove 1 to 2 cups to use as the test soil.

3 Use a purchased kit or take your soil to a testing laboratory. Some Cooperative Extension Service offices offer testing as a free service.

A GOOD START

You won't be able to mix sulfur into the soil after planting, so it's important to plan ahead to give your stewartia a good start. In all but alkaline soils, keeping the plant mulched with an acidic mulch and using a fertilizer designed for azaleas or camellias will be enough to maintain soil acidity.

JAPANESE SNOWBELL
Styrax japonica

Zones: 5–8

Type: Deciduous

Light: Full sun to part shade

Size: 20–30 ft. tall, 20–30 ft. wide

Form: Rounded to flat headed

Growth Rate: Moderate

Interest: Glossy green leaves in summer, yellow in fall; white bell-shaped flowers in spring

This excellent tree of slight proportions is most beautiful in full bloom in mid- to late spring. The open-branched canopy is full of white, starlike, open bells—dainty flowers that hang in small clusters below branches and leaves. The overall, mature structure is more horizontal than vertical, which adds to the charm of the floral display and gives Japanese snowbell a finely textured winter silhouette.

HOW TO GROW

Japanese snowbell is a bit fussy about soil. It needs acidic conditions, preferably well-drained loam high in organic matter. You should probably not attempt it in alkaline soil, but it is worth a try in sand or clay as long as there is ample moisture with no standing water. Light shade is best where summers are very hot, full sun elsewhere. Cold snaps in late spring sometimes damage leaves and stem tips, but the tree will recover. Try to avoid planting it in a cold pocket where damage is more likely.

LANDSCAPE USE

The strongly horizontal branching pattern of Japanese snowbell is picture-perfect summer and winter when set near a pond or pool, beside a patio or deck, or at the corner of a porch. If possible, plant it high so you can look up at the blossoms. Viewed from below, the open bells are highlighted by tiny tufts of yellow stamens in their centers. Japanese snowbell is at home in a mixed bed; the deep *Styrax* roots and light summer shade will not interfere with the other plants and the tree will benefit from any irrigation you give the bed.

Top Choices

- *S.* 'Pink Chimes' is similar in every way except for its delicate pink flowers. The weeping form, 'Carillon' (also called 'Pendula'), stays low and never reaches tree height.

- *S. obassia*, fragrant snowbell, hides its long, dangling panicles of highly fragrant blossoms under a cloak of 5- to 8-inch round leaves. This tree is as tall as *S. japonica*, but develops a vertical rather than horizontal form. It is less hardy and may show freeze damage below Zone 6.

CHOOSING A SMALL TREE

Small trees like Japanese snowbell are useful in solving some garden design problems. Though it eventually spreads a distance equal to its height (25 feet), you can fit it into a confined space by removing lower limbs and shortening exceptionally long side branches.

Consider any variety of Japanese snowbell for the following challenging situations:

- as a street tree under high-voltage lines that are only 35 feet above the ground;

- in a courtyard or small, streetside garden;

- as a background element for bulk but little shade against a building, wall, or fence;

- as an accent plant in a lawn against dark yews or other evergreens;

- for a small-scale grouping or grove with seasonal interest;

- as a moisture-tolerant focal point in a garden of constantly changing bedding plants;

- as a foreground plant to complement a taller, spring-flowering tree.

AMERICAN ARBORVITAE
Thuja occidentalis

Zones: 3–8

Type: Evergreen

Light: Full sun to light shade

Size: 30–40 ft. tall, 10–15 ft. wide

Form: Narrow pyramid branching to the ground

Growth Rate: Slow to moderate

Interest: Scalelike, flattened "needles"; tiny yellow to brown cones

Gardeners in the East may be surprised to learn that the 50- to 60-foot, sparsely foliaged white cedar in their local woods is the same species available in nurseries. Few cultivars ever exceed 30 feet in height, and many come in shades of blue, yellow, or gold. These dense, conical trees have short, twiggy limbs covered with fan-shaped sprays of scalelike foliage. When the flattened leaves are crushed or broken, they emit an herbal fragrance and an oil that causes a skin rash in some people.

HOW TO GROW
Arborvitae grows best in northern climates where it escapes intense summer heat. In hotter climates, it is shorter lived. Soil pH can range from slightly acidic to

slightly alkaline; other requirements include some humidity, good drainage, and full sun. If planted in heavy shade, this tree loses its compact shape and becomes loose, formless, and unattractive. Established plants will tolerate some heat, drought, and neglect; young trees establish fastest in fertile soil with plenty of moisture.

LANDSCAPE USE

Hardy and handsome, American arborvitae is one of the most useful trees for vertical effects. In northern climates especially, it is also one of the best privacy screens when planted in small groves or as a hedge. Shear hedges twice a year for best appearance, once in early summer and again in late summer. The dense branching extends to the ground and foliage is held year-round. Choose a cultivar with characteristics suited to its growing site in your landscape. Try to avoid any that turn brown in winter.

Top Choices

- *T.* 'Gold Cargo' has yellow foliage that resists browning in winter; it grows to 25 feet.

- *T.* 'Nigra' grows 20 to 30 feet tall while 'Techny' and 'Emerald' (also known as 'Smaragd') both grow to 15 feet tall. All hold green color through winter.

- *T.* 'Wintergreen' grows 20 to 30 feet tall and is dark green.

WINTER PROTECTION

Arborvitae trees with more than one main trunk are vulnerable to winter damage. Weight from accumulated ice and snow weighs down the vertical branches, bends them outward, and spoils the smooth outline. You can prevent damage by tying wires or nylon twine around trees in late fall and pulling vertical branches snugly inward.

Another protective method is to wire the tree loosely, but permanently. As the twiggy tips grow, foliage conceals the wire completely. Arborvitae is fairly slow growing, so wiring requires adjustment only every few years. On unwired trees, sweep snow off plants before it becomes too heavy for them to bear, being careful not to break branches in the process. You can avoid these winter problems by planting a single-trunked tree.

LITTLELEAF LINDEN
Tilia cordata

Zones: 3–7

Type: Deciduous

Light: Full sun

Size: 60–70 ft. tall, 30–50 ft. wide

Form: Densely pyramidal or oval and rounded

Growth Rate: Moderate to fast

Interest: Dark green, heart-shaped leaves, yellow in fall; dangling summer flowers and seeds

Littleleaf linden has long been a hands-down favorite shade tree in Europe and America. Its heart-shaped leaves are deep green above and paler beneath. Sweetly fragrant flowers, attractive to bees, appear in late spring to early summer, suspended on long stems but mostly inconspicuous within the foliage. For all-around use, it is hard to beat littleleaf linden.

HOW TO GROW

Linden is easy to grow and adapts to a wide range of conditions. Deep, rich soil with regular moisture is best; wet or dry compacted soil is worst. Linden withstands wind, polluted air in cities, and low fertility. Salt from winter streets and roadways may cause some leaf browning, but trees survive. Though generally disease resistant, some varieties attract insects, such as aphids. Use a strong hose jet to dislodge aphids and clean up the liquid—honeydew—they drop on surfaces below. In some areas, Japanese beetles may damage foliage.

LANDSCAPE USE

Littleleaf linden is a multipurpose tree, well suited for use as a street tree, shade tree, or lawn tree. Though individual leaves are small, shade may be too dense if you want to garden under the branches. In that case, keep lower branches pruned up, select a columnar variety, or plant a shade-tolerant ground cover. In a formal landscape, combine this tree with clipped boxwood hedges bordering a sweep of manicured lawn. Position several along a terrace or broad stone walk. Shape the trees into round or rectangular outlines, keeping a few individuals yards apart or several close enough so that the canopies merge.

Top Choices

- *T.* 'Chancellor' is fast growing and narrow, reaching about 30 feet.

- *T.* 'Greenspire' is also fast growing and has small leaves. It grows a bit taller—to 40 feet.

- *T.* 'Glenleven' bears the largest leaves.

- *T. tomentosa,* silver linden, is similar and offers a striking effect with foliage dark green above and silver below. It is hardy only to Zone 5.

- *T. t.* 'Pendula' is a weeping form.

- *T.* 'Sterling' resists the Japanese beetle.

SHEARING FOR EFFECT

Most sheared linden hedges appear in formal landscapes, but consider them a perfect choice for a tall privacy screen or a background to a courtyard, lawn, or border planting. Or plant them for an accent along a driveway. Wait at least one year after planting to begin training the hedge so the trees are growing vigorously.

1 In fall or during dormancy, cut back the central leader and lateral branches halfway to encourage bushiness.

2 When shoots reach the desired height and spread, trim them to shape each year.

3 Once the hedge is mature, you may want to shear only once a year in late summer.

CANADIAN HEMLOCK
Tsuga canadensis

Zones: 4–7

Type: Evergreen

Light: Full sun to full shade

Size: 40–70 ft. tall, 25–35 ft. wide

Form: Pyramidal

Growth Rate: Moderate

Interest: Short, flat, lustrous, dark green needles; small, dangling cones

One of the best conifers for shade, Canadian hemlock is also one of most beautiful of all evergreen trees. Graceful in youth and early maturity, it gains a rugged beauty in advanced age. In the forest, it reaches 90 feet and lives nearly a thousand years. In landscape situations it stays smaller. Hemlock's grandeur begins with lustrous, flattened needles, deep green above and bluish beneath, lining the sides of branchlets. Limbs on young trees are mostly horizontal, then curved and drooping as trees age.

HOW TO GROW
This conifer is most at home in a moist site. It needs loose, fast-draining, cool soil with constant access to moisture. During dry spells, give it supplemental irrigation. This is a

true forest denizen, not adapted to heat and aridity, pollution, salt, or heavy winds. Give it a protective environment, avoiding conditions on city streets; it is likely to fail in adverse conditions. Hemlock likes acidic soil, but this species seems to tolerate some alkalinity. It grows well in either sun or shade.

LANDSCAPE USE

One of the best uses for Canadian hemlock is as a hedge. It can be grown to any manageable height, but you can keep it as low as 3 feet. It makes a dense, fairly smooth, evergreen surface, valuable where cold tolerance is critical. Prune once in late spring or early summer; twice if growth is vigorous. (See "Shearing for Effect," page 113.) Renew poorly maintained hedges by pruning into old wood.

Canadian hemlock makes a marvelous specimen in a sheltered location. Plant one as an accent or several for a screen. Give each tree room to spread without interference from other trees. Use a group to frame a vista or define a space, such as separating an open lawn from a rougher area beyond.

Cool-Weather Start

Plant Canadian hemlock during the cool days of spring or fall. Check the soil diligently after planting to be sure that the rootball and the surrounding soil are equally moist. It will take several months before the roots take hold and growth begins.

SPECIALTY HEMLOCKS

Horticulturists have selected dozens of hemlocks from various *Tsuga* species for their particular mounded, weeping, or other interesting habit. Indeed, there seems to be a choice of color and size for every conceivable landscape role. Some of the best are slow-growing forms that have the potential to reach tree size but rarely do.

- *T.* 'Brandleyii' is slow growing with a nice, broadly pyramidal form.

- *T.* 'Hussi' is also slow growing, with dark green needles and an irregular form.

- *T.* 'Jervis' is pyramidal with especially dense branching.

- *T. caroliniana*, Carolina hemlock, is more compact, less flowing and graceful than Canadian hemlock. It is an equally good or better hedge plant and better for urban sites, since it isn't as fussy. It is, however, less cold tolerant. Zones 4 to 7.

- *T. heterophylla*, Western hemlock, thrives in its native Pacific Northwest and is the best species to plant there as a specimen tree, since it favors a cool maritime climate. A grand tree to 200 feet, it is imposing where space permits.

Japanese Elm
Zelkova serrata

Zones: 5–8

Type: Deciduous

Light: Full sun to light shade

Size: 50–80 ft. tall, 40–60 ft. wide

Form: Vase shaped with rounded crown

Growth Rate: Moderate to fast

Interest: Dark green leaves, mixed fall color; inconspicuous flowers and fruits; exfoliating bark

Tall, sturdy, and reminiscent of the stately American elm, Japanese elm has emerged as an impressive substitute for that disease-ravaged favorite. Leaves are dark green, toothed, rough, and strongly veined. Its fall color varies among individual trees from yellowish orange to rusty brown and purplish red. Smooth gray bark flakes off, leaving trunks mottled with russet, cream, and gray spots. Most trees have fairly short trunks that begin their vertical branching just a few feet above the ground.

How to Grow
Zelkova's only requirement is well-drained soil. It achieves its best growth in deep loam with regular water from rains or irrigation, but it grows well in average

conditions in sun or light shade, tolerating neglect and difficult sites. As a young tree grows, make sure the main trunk (the central leader) reaches at least 6 to 8 feet before it begins to branch. When it divides into several leaders, thin out the weakest to keep crotch angles open and the ascending structural limbs strong. The short, lower trunk will become quite stout with age. It is best to prune in fall or winter.

LANDSCAPE USE

Tall and stately, Japanese elm casts the same type of comfortable shade as true elm. The open branching makes it a good lawn or street tree—its principal uses, especially on large properties.

Top Choices

- Z. 'Green Vase' is a handsome, fast grower with distinctive vertical lines and vase shape.

- Z. 'Halka' is also fast growing, graceful, and exceptionally elmlike.

- Z. 'Village Green' has excellent fall color and improved cold hardiness. It shows a more rounded canopy than the other varieties and is the most resistant to insects and disease.

- Z. *sinica*, Chinese zelkova, is appropriate for smaller gardens. It reaches about 30 feet and is known to be more cold hardy.

SAFE TREE TRIMMING

When removing a limb from a large tree, cut it at its base rather than cutting it back partway. If the branch is long and heavy, bring in a professional arborist. If you're doing the job yourself, stand securely on a ladder or scaffolding above the work. Make three cuts:

1 Cut on the bottom side about 1 foot from the trunk and one-third through the limb.

2 Cut from the top a few inches farther out and clear through to sever the branch.

3 To remove the stub, make a final precision cut just outside the ridges of the branch collar. Never leave a stub or make a flush cut. Tissue around the collar expands to seal off exposed wood and prevent the entry of any damaging pests and diseases.

GLOSSARY

Acidic soil: Soil with a pH less than 7, common in climates with high rainfall.

Alkaline soil: Soil with a pH above 7, common in climates with low rainfall.

Bract: A leaflike structure often attached to the base of a flower, sometimes showy and appearing to be part of the flower, as in dogwood.

Candle: A budlike new shoot of a pine or other conifer, before the young needles expand.

Catkin: Dense and slender, often drooping, spike of flowers lacking petals; may be either male or female, as on birch trees.

Central leader: The primary upward-growing stem of a single-trunked tree.

Chlorosis: Yellowing of leaves caused by iron deficiency; often due to soil alkalinity preventing the uptake of iron.

Conifer: A cone-bearing tree or shrub, usually evergreen, with needles or scalelike foliage.

Cultivar: A cultivated variety produced through vegetative propagation or cloning, recognized by single quotes around its name, as in C. 'Rosea'.

Deciduous: Having leaves that drop off at one time each year; not evergreen.

Dormancy: A resting state when growth slows or stops, commonly during periods of reduced light and low temperatures in winter; for some species, during periods of intense heat and drought in summer.

Double flower: A flower with a greater number of petals than normal, giving it a full appearance.

Drip line: An imaginary line on the soil around a tree where water drips off the canopy, once thought to be the location of feeder roots. Most roots extend beyond the drip line.

Drupe: A berrylike fruit, such as a cherry, containing a seed in a hardened center that is surrounded by fleshy tissue.

Dwarf: Plant genetically identical to its species but shorter.

Evergreen: A woody plant that does not drop all of its leaves the same season.

Genus: Category of plants of closely related species.

Humus: Organic matter in the soil derived from the decomposition of animal and vegetable remains.

Hybrid: Plant from a cross most often between two species or varieties.

Leaf scorch: Browning of leaf edges and centers caused by rapid loss of moisture (or chemical dehydration), often resulting in leaf drop.

Leaflet: A part of a compound leaf that in itself resembles a leaf.

Lenticel: A pore on a woody stem for the exchange of gases; commonly a small bump; variously a conspicuous striation, as on cherry bark.

Lime: Soil amendment containing calcium, used to raise soil pH to reduce acidity and increase alkalinity.

Loam: A natural blend of clay, silt, and sand rich in organic matter.

Mulch: Protective material spread over soil to control weeds, conserve moisture, protect roots, moderate soil temperature, and prevent erosion.

Neutral: Soil with a pH of 7, neither acid nor alkaline.

Node: That part of a stem where buds, leaves, or branches are attached.

Organic matter: Decomposed material originating from plants or animals.

Palmate: Radiating outward from a point, like the fingers on a hand.

Panicle: Multi-branched flower cluster that blooms from the bottom to the top.

pH: An expression of the hydrogen ion content of soil to indicate its relative acidity or alkalinity.

Pinnate: Arranged featherlike along a main axis or stalk.

Rachis: The stalk or axis of a compound leaf to which leaflets are attached.

Rootstock: The lower part of a grafted plant including the roots; also, an underground stem, a rhizome.

Sepal: One of the outermost parts surrounding a flower, usually enclosing the bud; leaflike then folding back after opening, sometimes petal-like, as in daylily.

Shrub: Woody perennial, usually multi-stemmed from the ground level or near it, and smaller than a tree.

Single flower: A flower possessing the minimum number of petals for its kind, usually four, five, or six.

Species: Group of closely related individuals that can breed together and produce similar offspring.

Specimen: A single, prominently placed plant with highly valued ornamental features.

Spike: Single-stemmed flower cluster in which each flower lacks a stalk.

Spreading: Growing laterally or horizontally by elongation of branches from the main stem.

Stamen: The male, pollen-bearing part of a flower, often long, slender, and in groups in the center of a flower.

Sucker: Shoot arising from underground, usually from roots and often from grafted rootstock.

Tepals: Undifferentiated sepals and petals, as in magnolia flowers.

Variety: Subdivision of a species consistently showing differences throughout generations.

Vegetative propagation: Production of a new plant through a method other than growing from seeds, such as layering, cuttings, division, or grafting.

Witches' broom: Distorted, twiggy growths at the ends of branches.

Whorl: A group of three or more leaves, flowers, or branches encircling a stem at a single node.

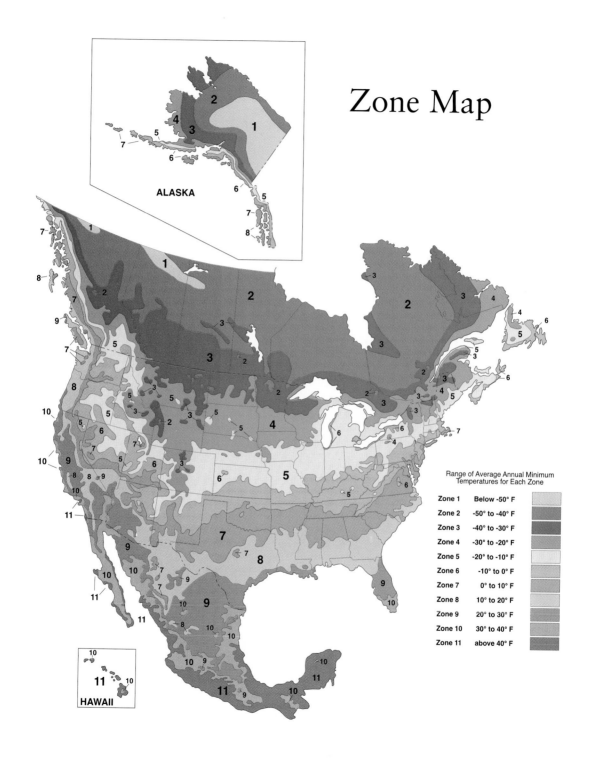

Zone Map

ALASKA

HAWAII

Range of Average Annual Minimum
Temperatures for Each Zone

Zone 1	Below -50° F
Zone 2	-50° to -40° F
Zone 3	-40° to -30° F
Zone 4	-30° to -20° F
Zone 5	-20° to -10° F
Zone 6	-10° to 0° F
Zone 7	0° to 10° F
Zone 8	10° to 20° F
Zone 9	20° to 30° F
Zone 10	30° to 40° F
Zone 11	above 40° F

Photography & Illustration Credits

INDEX

*Page numbers in italics refer
to illustrations.*

Storey Communications, Inc.
Pownal, Vermont

President: M. John Storey
Executive Vice President: Martha M. Storey
Chief Operating Officer: Dan Reynolds
Director of Custom Publishing: Deirdre Lynch
Project Manager: Barbara Weiland
Author: Rosemary McCreary
Book Design: Betty Kodela
Design Assistance: Jen Rork
Horticultural Edit: Liz Stell; Charles W. G. Smith